The Ultimate Beginner's Guide to Raising a Happy Akita

A Simple, Practical Guide to Akita Care, Training, Nutrition, and Having the Happiest Akita in Town

By
Jessica Williams

3

TABLE OF CONTENTS

5

INTRODUCTION

I was absolutely stunned when I saw my first Akita
-- pronounced AH' kee ta by the Japanese and Ah
Kee' ta by most Americans.

These magnificent imposing dogs' great heads make
them look like young bears – or foxes -- while their
large-boned bodies and curly tails say they're
descended from Spitz-type dogs – the kind that
existed about 15,000 years ago during the Stone Age.

In 1931, after realizing that the Akita was fast
becoming extinct, Japan declared the Japanese Akita
a Japanese National Treasure.

In fact, the Akita has had a bumpy ride in terms of
survival as a breed.

As the Akita ran the gamut from primitive times' use
as a hunting, weight bearing working dog through
the centuries until today, he was cross bred a
number of times. He was systematically hunted and
killed during some eras. He was cross bred in others

for some unique reasons.

Because of this repeated cross breeding, there are very few true representatives of the two strains of Japanese Akitas to be found.

One is the Ichoneski; the other, the Dewa.
The first was short and heavy boned; the second medium boned and taller.

The most famous of the Dewa line was Kongo-Go, owned by the late Mr. Heihacki Hashimoto. Kongo-Go was used to breed dogs in America; Kongo-Go's ancestors may show up today in the fourth or fifth generation on breed papers.

Today, you may find a Japanese type Akita or an American type. We'll look at the dog's standards shortly.

For now, it's a good beginning for you to know that the Akita, with its intelligent, warm, loving calm if dominant personality; its loyalty to his human family and his natural tendency to protect; its relative easiness to train; and its ability to survive alone if necessary, makes it an unusual and attractive breed.

However, you really need to know and understand this breed before you take one home with you.

This comprehensive guide to knowing, buying and caring for an Akita – warts and all – will help you make an educated decision – and, if you already own one, hopefully help you to know and understand him even better.

Note: I will mostly use the male gender to mean both genders: Please forgive any slight you may feel to your Lady Suki. I mean to avoid tangling the reader up in s/he's and such. But I promise to honor your Lady when it is clear we are talking about a female Akita. I'm trying, folks.

CHAPTER 1:
The Akita, From Yesterday to Today

Akitas are large dogs, averaging 24 to 28 inches at their shoulders and weighing from 80 to over 100 pounds. Female Akitas usually weigh about 80 pounds or so.
Japanese pure bred Akitas are shorter with more defined and smaller frames.

Akitas are dog–aggressive which means that he will attack strange animals and even those dogs in his own family if they are Akitas of the same gender, of if they join the household after he does.

He is not known to be people aggressive but he can be aggressive to children.

He is a hunter who will consider wildlife, cats, and small dogs, etc. as prey and so cannot be left to roam around the neighborhood alone and off leash.

Experienced breeders believe he should NEVER be

off leash.

One owner said jokingly that her Akita is never allowed near her chicken coops because Akitas have been bred to see them as dinner without the gravy.

Akitas are large and imposing and bred from ancient times to be dominant.

On the other hand, your Akita may be a silly billy, playing little games with you like holding your hand in his mouth and leading you gently to what he wants you to see, or even playing jokes on his family like bumping them a little when they are not looking.

Akitas, who rarely bark, talks to his loved ones. He woos them with little sounds that may seem like growls until you know him. They are not. His little low noises are his way of "billing and cooing" with you. It won't be long before you recognize his different sounds.

And for such a large working dog, they are very docile.

However, they are very protective of their loved ones, and can be aggressive when doing that.

One breeder said about one of her beloved Akitas: "When someone strange comes near, she comes very close and leans up against me, watching. It's like she wants to make sure she is between me and anyone who might want to hurt me."

For a happy successful relationship with an Akita, it's important for Akita owners to understand their Akita's personality and needs.

THE AKITA'S NUMBER ONE NEEDS ARE TO HAVE AN ALPHA PACK LEADER – YOU -- AND VERY GOOD OBEDIENCE TRAINING.

And, because an Akita can be a dominant kind of dog, and because he weighs more than most children or even a small adult, and because he is territorial – especially about his food – and protective of his family, training cannot be a slapdash "maybe he does, maybe he doesn't" kind of training.

Let me put that another way.

Its master or mistress cannot be permissive. With an Akita, what you put into his training is what you get out as his behavior.

The positive side of the Akita, Japanese or American type, is that he is naturally protective of his family; he is faithful and loyal, and he can live with other animals and children safely and happily given the right training and socialization.

He is docile and adjusts easily to any environment and lifestyle. He is an affectionate animal who often demonstrates a charming sense of humor.

He's also a brilliant animal who seems to be able to think.

"The Akita can think and even when he's doing what you want him to do, you can see by the way he holds his ears and the expression on his face that he's thinking of how to get away with not doing it," said another Akita breeder.

In other words, he's a brilliant animal with a complex personality.

Doesn't that sound like some humans we know?

Now, isn't it true that when you decide to spend your life with another living creature – human or Akita – that you need to know all there is to know about your new companion BEFORE you make the move?

Providing you with that important information is my goal in writing this book.

The Akita – An Inspiration

As a writer, the first thing I thought when I saw this impressive Akita, was, "I need to write about this dog so people will know how to get one and keep one."

The Akita is a faithful, lovable and loving dog and I understand your attraction and interest in this noble animal.

However, with animals as with people, one kind doesn't suit all.

Honestly, the first thing I thought when I saw this impressive looking animal on the other end of a gal's leash one day was, "I can see why someone might get one of these just because they attract so much attention or just because it's kind of trendy."

And then the gal and I started to talk about her much loved Akita and I started to wonder how hard it would be to raise and train one.

And how I would know how to pick out the right one for me.

I am terminally curious as you can probably tell. So

when I got home that evening, I started reading everything I could find about the Akita (there are now two types according to the authority clubs.) and tracked down trainers and well known breeders of both types.

And ultimately went on to check it out with other experts – the best ones I could find.

And fell in love with this primitive dog and its amazing history and temperament.

I learned that the more you know about this special primitive dog called the Akita, the more you respect him and the easier it will be to choose the right one.

Everything You've Always Wanted to Know About Akitas is here for you to use as a reference book for before and after you get YOUR Akita.

It even includes a few tricks you will both enjoy learning together.

"Traveling With Your Akita" is meant to help you travel with or ship your Akita safely and pleasantly. It even includes how to travel by airplane, not an easy feat given the Akita's size and reputation as a power breed.

A bonus feature is a check list of questions you can ask breeders to help you choose YOUR Akita.

Another bonus feature is a list of some quick and easy tricks you can teach your Akita, a playtime game you will both enjoy.

Why you need a good guide book BEFORE you get your Akita

The Akita is a loving dog with an impressive history. Amazingly, he is also the easiest of all primitive dogs to train.

You can housebreak an Akita puppy in weeks.

Now doesn't that make you happy?

However, there's a lot more to know about the Akita.

And having the right information about the Akita can help you judge the Akitas and breeders. Yes, I said breeders -- plural.

You need to talk to a few breeders and meet some Akitas, see a show that has Akitas in it, and "meet" a few Akitas. All this BEFORE you plunk down your dollars for a wonderful little ball of fur with a Teddy bear or Foxy face.

That 20 pound fluffy cutie will grow large enough and strong enough to backpack part of your camping supplies into the woods or pull a sled.
When adults, Akitas are able to carry 30 percent of their weight on their backs.

I want you to be happy with your Akita if you decide, after learning all about one, that he is in fact your kind of dog.

That, with the right training and socialization, he will be your best buddy, most faithful animal companion, just the smartest, most loyal creature you've ever had by your side for 24/7.

You should want to fight to the nth to get him and keep him forever.

Okay, I confess. I am writing this for you AND for your Akita.

One of the worse tragedies of impulsive dog buying is how the dogs may suffer.

Many puppies, bought when they are cute and

cuddly, are all too often abandoned when they grow up. And many, by the time they are brought to a shelter or found on a country road, hungry and frightened, are labeled unadoptable. We all know what that means.

However, with the right training and socialization, you will develop a long term companionship that will benefit you both.

An Akita has a long life span -- from 10 to 12 years is not unusual, with some few longevity champs make it to 14 years – so you will have time to build a significant relationship with your Akita. She will become a close friend and protector in your life, your family's life, and perhaps even your community's life.

How about thinking of the following few questions as you read the next chapters that tell you Everything You've Always Wanted to Know About Akitas.

Is this your first dog?

Why do you want an Akita?

Do you want a show dog, a pet, or both? (At home, a show dog will be a pet, right?)

Do you want a puppy or an older dog?

Can you give him the home and environment he needs?

Since the Akita prefers to live in the house with his family, ask yourself: do you have room for such a large roommate?

Do you have a yard that needs fencing? It has to be over 6 feet high or higher or away he will go.

Are you committed to the cost of raising and keeping a large and powerful dog like the Akita?

Are you committed to giving him the kind of training he will need to keep you happy with him?

Do you have little children in the home and if so, are you committed to training them how to properly and safely relate to an Akita? Hint: They need to be gentle with this gentle giant.

Do you have other animals in the home? If they are small dogs, how will they relate to the puppy Akita? And then, later, to the large full grown Akita?

Are you committed to having your Akita spayed or

neutered at an early age? This helps reduce any aggressive tendencies and protects his or her health so you both benefit.

How will the Akita relate to other animals in the house?

Before you make the absolute final move and go out meeting breeders, let's get down to the nitty gritty.

Let us tell you Everything You Ever Wanted to Know About an Akita.

Learning all you can about the Akita and his needs will give you a good check list for the day you start looking at Akitas and choosing your special new friend.

CHAPTER 2:
Ancient History of the Honorable Akita-Inu

The Japanese term Akita-Inu translates literally into Akita-Dog.

The history of the Japanese Akita's existence and its breeding throughout the past three and one-half centuries is as fascinating a tale as the appearance of the almond-eyed Akita itself.

It includes mystery, romance, tragedy, horrors, courage, and of course, the Akita's incredible beauty.

During the Stone Age in prehistoric Japan, nomads crossed from Siberia into Alaska and Japan, bringing with them large hunting dogs. Archeological digs in the Jonan Period, about 10,000 years ago, found evidence of dogs with the usual characteristics of large dogs traveling with primitive people, similar in size and type to Akitas.

But it was not yet the Akita we know of today.

It was only when the land masses split, creating isolated islands, that this Spitz-type dog gained its distinct features.

His name, by the way, is derived from his home region of Akita, on the island of Honshu.

Just imagining the many centuries this special breed has walked the earth is mind-boggling, isn't it?

What has the Akita – a working dog -- done throughout his history?

It seems there is no limit to the services he's provided: the Akita has been used throughout the centuries for everything a large courageous dog can be used to do!

Male and female Akita teams of two were once used to hunt and ferret out bears. To corner them and keep them at bay until hunters arrived.

Not just any bears, but the Mother and Father of all bears. The Yezo bear weighed in at about 800 pounds, and that's a lot of bear to keep cornered.

On the other hand, Akitas have been used to fetch killed waterfowl; they have surprisingly tender mouths.

With exquisitely careful and proper training, they can be used to hunt large wild animals even today.

This is not to be attempted by the average Akita owner. A hunting team's training is very sophisticated and absolutely necessary. He also needs an orange hunting vest. Just think: If a human can accidentally shoot another human, imagine how easy it would be to accidentally kill an animal that looks like a large wolf or fox!

The Akita has been a guard dog and a sled dog.

He has even been used occasionally s a police dog.

The Akita is a living contradiction.

Known as an imposing dog who can intimidate the toughest, he is also a docile dog who will do anything for affection.

In fact, the Akita has its feline side; he will wash his face after meals just like a cat does with his tight paws, and pad quietly around the house, cat-fashion.

27

It is said he has strong dominant characteristics and demands an alpha master or mistress, yet according to Japanese myth, when a baby is born, a little statue of an Akita is sent to her parents as a happiness and health symbol.

Tragically, during the periods when dog fighting was the "in" thing in samurai circles, the Akita was crossbred with the toughest known fighting dog in Japan at that time – the Tosa -- and probably imported mastiffs.

This created an even larger Akita with much more aggressive tendencies. And muddied his breeding lines for a long time.

Another tragedy to befall the Akita-Inu was World War II.

In Japan, the cold weather and the hunger of war torn Japan combined to make the Akita the hunted instead of the hunter.

Akitas were hunted down and killed in very large numbers for food and their pelts which were used to make warm clothing for the military.

In fact, all Japanese dogs were ordered to be found and confiscated by the Japanese government during WWII. Only German Shepherds were spared.

I'll bet you know exactly what happened then.

If you said they were then cross bred with German Shepherds in an attempt to save them, you are right on target.

Others, it's been said, were saved by Akita owners who shipped them to far-off mountains where authorities were told they were needed as wartime pack animals.

The Akita as a National Monument

In 1931, Japan's Ministry of Education, noting the threat of Akita extinction, declared purebred Akitas a National Monument.

They became the largest of seven Japanese dogs to be awarded this title.

The others are: the medium sized Hokkaido-Inu, Kai-Inu, Shidodu-Inu, Kishi-Inu, Shikoku-Inu, and the small Shiba-Inu.

The AKC first permitted the Akita to register with them in 1972.

The Akita Club of America was founded in 1956.

As we've said, the Akita has had its good and bad times.

Three things helped save the Akita from breed extinction.

One is a tender story of an Akita's noble love for his master that became an inspiration to all of Japan.

The story goes: In the 1930s, Hachi-Ko, an Akita whose master, Dr. Elisaburo, was a professor at Tokyo University, accompanied him daily to the Shibuya train station on Tokyo's Yamanote line.

After the train left, so did Hachi-Ko who then returned to the train station each evening to meet his master as he returned from his city university job.

One evening, Hachi-Ko waited and waited, but his master did not come.

Each day, for the following 9 years, Hachi-Ko returned to the train station and sat there through sun and rain, year after year, waiting for his master, who had died suddenly at the university.

Japanese people, from the smallest child to the most elderly, were moved by the story of Hachi-Ko and his immense loyalty.

After Hachi-Ko died, a statue of the incredibly loyal Akita was cast in bronze and placed at the train station.

Although it was melted down during WWII for use in the government's metal seeking efforts, another statue of Hachi-Ko was installed later that you can see, still sitting at the train station.

Helen Keller and Kamikazi

The Akita's second claim to fame happened when Ms. Helen Keller, who overcame being born both blind and deaf to become one of our most revered Americans, visited Japan in the late 1930s.

Her joyous spirit and warmth were so impressive that a police officer who owned a tiny Akita puppy sent it to her as a gift.

It was the first Akita ever brought to America.

Although Ms. Keller's dog named Kamikazi died of distemper soon after, a second Akita -- Kenzan-Go – was sent to her by her Japanese fans and became her constant companion.

The American GI and the Akita

The third assistance to some kind of continuity for Akitas was the ingenuity of the American GI.

During WWII, American military men saw them, were impressed by these imposing animals and according to Akita legend, smuggled large numbers of them into America with them when they returned from the war.

Other allied servicemen did the same but it was in America that the passion for these special dogs quickly soared.

Those GI sponsored Akitas became the early gene pool for the popular American Akita that quickly popped up in pet shops everywhere after their arrival in America.

The kind the GIs brought back were the larger "fighting dog" type of Akita/Shepherd mix "Akitas."

What is the Modern Akita?

During the first half of the 1900s, two types of dogs were called Akitas: the Matagi Akita or hunting dog, and Tosa fighting Akita, which we've already mentioned as having been cross bred with mastiffs and other large dogs like the Great Dane and the German Shepherd.

Up to the 1970s, the types brought to America were the fighting and Shepherd mix kind of Akitas. They became wildly popular with American buyers and were the kind seen in pet shops.

They were known as The American Akita.

Two different Akitas

The proliferation of these larger animals bred of fighting stock and mixed with German Shepherds and mastiffs confused breeders and show organizations immensely. They were American Akitas, but were they Japanese Akitas?

"Even in Japan there was not total agreement as to

what constituted the true Akita," reported Sophia Kaluzniacki, DVM and Akita expert.

"There were five organizations, all with their own standard promoting their version of the breed. The dominant one, today the parent club for the breed in Japan, is known as AKIHO. Largely through the efforts of this club and its breeders, the Akita in Japan changed dramatically from the dog found right after WWII," she reported in the late 90s.

For those new to the world of pedigree and show dogs, standards are lists of a special breed's ideal specifications. Show judges use these standards to decide which dog comes closest to the ideal. Standards are created by the breed's organizations.

Legend says that after Japanese breeders agreed that the true Akita is the Matagi or hunting type, they carefully cross bred Akitas until they had brought back the true Matagi type Akita.

After two Akita world conferences, the last held in Germany in 1998, it was decided to recognize two official breeds of the Akita.

The American Akita is now officially called The Great American Dog in Fédération Cynologique Internationale (FCI) countries while the Japanese Akita retained the title of Japanese Akita.

The FCI is the World Canine Organization. Its members and partners represent 80 countries. Each issues its own pedigrees and prepares their own judges. One of its roles is to recognize standards and so it played an important role in defining Akitas as two separate breeds.

In America, however, the two Akita types are considered one breed. This is a controversial issue even today.

The Two Akitas and their standards

When the American Kennel Club began to register Akitas in 1972, it adopted the standards from the AKIHO – the Akita-Inu Preservation Society. Therefore, the two dogs' standards were – and are according to the AKC – the same.

However, as Japanese Akita breeder Pat Szymanski says, "The standards remain the same but the American Akita and the Japanese Akita are different dogs."

We'll talk about a few differences between the two Akitas after the AKC standards' segment of this book.

Knowing what you want in YOUR Akita from the get-go will help you find the right breeder, choose YOUR

Akita up close and personal, and have some clues what to expect from your Akita as he or she grows up.

AMERICAN KENNEL CLUB

Akita Breed Standard
Working Group

General Appearance
Large, powerful, alert, with much substance and heavy bone. The broad head, forming a blunt triangle, with deep muzzle, small eyes and erect ears carried forward in line with back of neck, is characteristic of the breed. The large, curled tail, balancing the broad head, is also characteristic of the breed.

Head
Massive but in balance with body; free of wrinkle when at ease. Skull flat between ears and broad; jaws square and powerful with minimal dewlap. Head forms a blunt triangle when viewed from above. *Fault*--Narrow or snipy head. *Muzzle*--Broad and full. Distance from nose to stop is to distance from stop to occiput as 2 is to 3. *Stop*--Well defined, but not too abrupt. A shallow furrow extends well up forehead. *Nose*--Broad and black. Liver permitted on white Akitas, but black always preferred. *Disqualification*--Butterfly nose or total lack of pigmentation on nose. *Ears*--The ears of the Akita are characteristic of the breed. They are strongly erect and small in relation to rest of head. If ear is

folded forward for measuring length, tip will touch upper eye rim. Ears are triangular, slightly rounded at tip, wide at base, set wide on head but not too low, and carried slightly forward over eyes in line with back of neck. *Disqualification*--Drop or broken ears. *Eyes*--Dark brown, small, deep-set and triangular in shape. Eye rims black and tight. *Lips and Tongue*--Lips black and not pendulous; tongue pink. *Teeth*--Strong with scissors bite preferred, but level bite acceptable. *Disqualification*--Noticeably undershot or overshot.

Neck and Body
Neck--Thick and muscular; comparatively short, widening gradually toward shoulders. A pronounced crest blends in with base of skull. *Body*--Longer than high, as 10 is to 9 in males; 11 to 9 in bitches. Chest wide and deep; depth of chest is one-half height of dog at shoulder. Ribs well sprung, brisket well developed. Level back with firmly-muscled loin and moderate tuck-up. Skin pliant but not loose. *Serious Faults*--Light bone, rangy body.

Tail
Large and full, set high and carried over back or against flank in a three-quarter, full, or double curl, always dipping to or below level of back. On a three-quarter curl, tip drops well down flank. Root large and strong. Tail bone reaches hock when let down. Hair coarse, straight and full, with no appearance of a plume. *Disqualification*--Sickle or uncurled tail.

Forequarters and Hindquarters
Forequarters--Shoulders strong and powerful with moderate layback. Forelegs heavy-boned and

straight as viewed from front. Angle of pastern 15 degrees forward from vertical. *Faults*--Elbows in or out, loose shoulders. *Hindquarters*--Width, muscular development and bone comparable to forequarters. Upper thighs well developed. Stifle moderately bent and hocks well let down, turning neither in nor out. *Dewclaws*--On front legs generally not removed; dewclaws on hind legs generally removed. *Feet*--Cat feet, well knuckled up with thick pads. Feet straight ahead.

Coat

Double-coated. Undercoat thick, soft, dense and shorter than outer coat. Outer coat straight, harsh and standing somewhat off body. Hair on head, legs and ears short. Length of hair at withers and rump approximately two inches, which is slightly longer than on rest of body, except tail, where coat is longest and most profuse. *Fault*--Any indication of ruff or feathering.

Color

Any color including white; brindle; or pinto. Colors are brilliant and clear and markings are well balanced, with or without mask or blaze. White Akitas have no mask. Pinto has a white background with large, evenly placed patches covering head and more than one-third of body. Undercoat may be a different color from outer coat.

Gait

Brisk and powerful with strides of moderate length. Back remains strong, firm and level. Rear legs move in line with front legs.

Size
Males 26 to 28 inches at the withers; bitches 24 to 26 inches. *Disqualification*--dogs under 25 inches; bitches under 23 inches.

Temperament
Alert and responsive, dignified and courageous. Aggressive toward other dogs.

Disqualifications
Butterfly nose or total lack of pigmentation on nose.
Drop or broken ears.
Noticeably undershot or overshot.
Sickle or uncurled tail.
Dogs under 25 inches; bitches under 23 inches.

Approved December 12, 1972

The most dramatic difference between the two Akitas of today is the difference between the two Akitas' heads.

The larger-boned American Akita, with its large triangular head and small eyes, shows a remarkable resemblance to a bear.

The Japanese Akita-Inu's head, with its almond eyes and ears set lower and more forward than the American Akita's, resembles the head of an over-sized fox.

The American Akita can be any color; sometimes the

undercoat has a different color than the upper coat. They mostly have black masks. They were traditionally bred to be guard dogs.

Japanese Inu's colors are limited to brindle, white, and red with white markings.
The Japanese Akita-Inu was bred to be a companion dog. Even so, the two Akitas have similar temperaments. Personalities depend on the individual dog.

If you prefer the smaller boned dog with the fox face, and want to have a pure bred Japanese type dog, the Japanese Akita-Inu is one you will want to seek out for you and your family.

If you prefer the larger American Akita with its astonishing resemblance to a bear and its fascinating historical cross breeding, you will seek out a breeder who specializes in this type of Akita.

DNA, the Akita, and the Ancient Wolf

For those readers fascinated, as I am, in the Akita's history, recent scientific research on the "genetic fingerprints" of some 85 types of purebred canines offers a more defined look at the Akita's genetic connection to a wolf.

In 2004, a scientific study of these 85 breeds,

financed in part by the American Kennel Club, found that 14 breeds are 99 percent identified as "ancient." This means that those 14 have been genetically defined by DNA as being closer to wolves than other dogs.

Does this mean they are temperamentally or physically LIKE wolves? No, no, and no.

Elaine Ostrander, a geneticist at the Fred Hutchinson Cancer Research Center and University of Washington in Seattle, co-directed the study with Leonid Kruglyak. She told Mark Derr of the New York Times News Service that while the study can pinpoint a dog to a breed, researchers do not have the capability yet to tell what behavior or appearance the dog will have.

The DNA/Canine research was published on May 21, 2004 in the journal *Science Volume 304*. It is expected to help in the study of canine and human disease.

The 14 primitive breeds identified to date include the Akita, Alaskan Malamute, Afghan Hound, Basenji, Chow Chow, Lhasa Apso, Pekingese, Saluki, Samoyed, Shar-Pei, Shibu-Inu, Shih Tzu, Siberian Husky, and the Tibetan Terrier.

CHAPTER 3:
The Akita Temperament - A Personality and Mind of Its Own

Understanding an Akita is a challenge. As I said earlier, he is a living Japanese monument – and a wonderful loving, living contradiction.

He is faithful and loving and naturally protective of his family yet he can also be a dangerous dog if some cautions are not followed.

While the Akita is an aggressive dog by breed, he is also a docile dog for owners who are Alpha Pack Leaders.

People who would be permissive with their dog are not going to be able to control an Akita. You need to be able to gain respect from your Akita. That respect will convince your dog that he MUST obey you.

Remember, while he will be easy for you to pick up

or move around when he is a 20 pound puppy, the Akita grows so rapidly that he will quickly be a huge dog. It is not unusual for a 7 month Akita to weigh 95 pounds or more!

However, a professional breeder can help acquaint you with their dogs' characteristics, their personal quirks and how to deal with the one you choose to some extent. They will know the sire and dam's personalities and can somewhat predict how their personalities might be forwarded to their litters.

A professional breeder who takes pride in their Akitas may also be able to help you decide which of the litter may be the one most suited to you -- and the puppy's new environment.

An Akita has this happy ability to adjust easily to any environment or lifestyle. That is a giant plus.

Still, he is dog-aggressive. This means that he is not able to be housed with another dog of the same gender, and sometimes not with one of the opposite gender.

He may do better with another dog in the same home if the other dog was there before him and is the same gender as the Akita.

Or he may not. If you have another dog in the home, it's best if you keep them apart when you are not there to supervise them. This is when the Akita's crate will come in handy. He does not mind being in it. He sees it as his sanctuary.

Here's a tip from a long time breeder of Japanese Akitas: Even if the Akita seems to dote on your little Poodle, do NOT leave them in the house alone while you go out. Sad things have been known to happen under those circumstances.

While the Akita is aggressive towards other dogs, he is not normally people aggressive.

However, experts agree that Akitas should NEVER be left alone with an unsupervised child.

When your Akita is properly trained and socialized, he will allow his family's children to play with him, even ride him like their big pony without objection. The Akita will simply roam off when he gets tired of this game.

Nevertheless, accidents can happen. Akitas do not like to be teased. And their reaction will be aggressive. That may mean he may growl – or he may BITE.

Therefore, all children – even those he seems to love dearly, should always be supervised when with the Akita.

And any time a strange child is visiting your child, the Akita should ALWAYS be put into his locked crate and kept there until the visiting child leaves.

Children may roughhouse or scream or play in a way that arouses your Akita's protective feelings towards his Child – yours -- and could attack the other child.

Now, I've heard owners joyously relate how their Akita loves strange children and this could be true in general, but it is breed specific that Akitas are prone to be aggressive to unknown children.

In addition, dogs that attack others can be euthanized by court order.

Some breeders will not sell an Akita to families with small children. And all ethical and careful breeders vet their potential clients whose aim is a companion dog.

Here is a mantra for you when judging when to be more cautious with your Akita than other times: BETTER SAFE THAN SORRY.

On the other hand, if all this sounds a bit intimidating, you might like to know that Akitas are owned and appreciated greatly by many families and a number of celebrities: Cher, Cal Ripken, Jr., Sarah Michelle Geller, Yoko Ono and Dan Ackroyd are just a few.

Training and common sense cautions for this particular breed are the keys to owning and enjoying the Akitas.

The Good News about the Akita

One very important thing you might consider: Early spaying or neutering decreases the Akita's aggressive tendencies.

The Akita is very smart and seems to be able to THINK, according to its breeders and owners.

HE IS TRAINABLE.

For the right master and home, he is a faithful, affectionate, funny, sweet dog who will protect you and your home and family and require no special training to do so.

However, he's also so smart that he can get bored and walk off from training exercises just as you think things are rolling along beautifully.

Ho Hum, he's just bored.

He's not stubborn. He's not wayward. He's not spiteful. He's just bored.

An Akita's training must be done in small segments – ten minutes at a time will be more productive than trying to push him into doing 20 minutes.

Don't be surprised if he simply walks off after ten minutes. That's an Akita. He's not trying to be boss or being stubborn or spiteful; he's just bored with the same old thing.

Check out the training segment of this book for tips on how to train your Akita.

But here's training tip number one, tip number two, AND tip number one hundred.

The Akita's trainer – and that should be YOU -- needs to demonstrate Clarity, Consistency, and PATIENCE.

Akitas are very social animals. They crave affection and attention. The more you gently handle the puppy, the better adult dog you will have.

The Akita is an in the house dog. He is slow and quiet moving -- basically a couch potato rather than a Russell Terrier Zip Around.

Ironically, this large dog, capable of feats of strength, is in many ways like a cat. Quiet, clean, with no odor. He even cleans his face with his paws after he eats. Isn't THAT something?

He does not do well as an outside dog. As a rule, they can, when trained properly, be given the run of the house as adults. They can even use a dog door without problems.

Akita puppies will do some chewing so put away your expensive brief case or the baby's swing while you are out. When they chew, they chew BIG time. Like all puppies, they usually outgrow their chewing phase after about a year.

He can even live happily in an apartment as long as someone exercises him for 30 to 60 minutes or so a day.

Please don't get an Akita if you are not able or willing to have him live indoors. Neither of you will be happy nor will the relationship work out.

He's very territorial – especially about his food and belongings.

And because an Akita is dog-aggressive, you need to skip any dog park visits.

"You can be walking with your dog and a person will come up and the dog will lick his hand but if that person is walking another dog, your Akita could attack him because he has a strong prey instinct," said an Akita breeder.

They should NEVER be taken to a dog park is the consensus of Akita trainers and breeders.

Said one, "Dog parks are not natural. Dogs are not meant to run with all these other dogs, large and small. It is not they way dogs have been bred over the years. Akitas should never be taken to a dog park."

Follow the leash laws ALL THE TIME.

What some owners say about their Akitas

I cannot tell a lie. I shamelessly snooped through Akita forums and chat rooms to eavesdrop on Akita owners as they talked about their Akitas. My undercover operation was intended to get the absolute scoop on the Akita from the folks who would know best: owners who live with Akitas 24/7.

For copy write reasons, I cannot quote these dog owners. However, I can share with you their opinions about their Akitas. I hope that will give you some special insights into the breed.

K lives with three dogs, one an Akita and is delighted with its "sunny personality."

Another owner makes it clear that he is in tune with both the view of an Akita as a docile animal and those who consider it an aggressive animal. He has known two Akitas from the same litter and sees the difference between the two males. One, he says, is "laid back" and the other untouchable by strangers.

Other forum posters say that training makes the difference; that they should always be kept on a leash; and that being a strong Alpha who also offers lots of affection will give you a great Akita.

Frankly, there are as many opinions about the Akita's temperaments and needs as there are Akita owners. Check into an Akita forum or two and just "lurk" for awhile. It is a great way to

learn about the Akita. And maybe make a friend
or two.

Adopting an Akita from a Rescue Group

There are a number of excellent states and a national
rescue group that specialize in rescuing Akitas of all
ages.

I am very pleased that there are such groups to care
for this great animal who may be a sweet lovable guy
or gal whose family had other reasons than the dog's
personality for rejecting him.

Many people have adopted Akitas with great success
and now have a warm relationship with their Akita.

If you plan to do that, here are a few guidelines to
consider before taking a rescued Akita into your
home.

Do not adopt an Akita from a dog shelter or adoption
center where you can't meet the dog's former owner
and/or know all there is to know about the dog. If
there is ANY vagueness about the dog's history, <u>walk
away from that dog</u>.

If the dog has already been trained to be a guard dog,

leave it there no matter how handsome it is, or how much you think you want a guard dog. Akitas are natural guard dogs. Anyone who tries to train them to be a guard dog has created a dangerous animal. Walk away.

And it goes without saying that you NEVER take an unknown Akita into an environment where there are children.

Again, "Better safe than sorry."

Getting the Perfect Akita for YOU

Six things you can do to get the perfect Akita for YOU:

1. Read this book carefully and carefully consider each fact it presents about the Akita as it relates to your and your household *as it exists now*. Don't' plan to change your lifestyle to fit the dog; it won't likely happen.

2. Decide which kind of Akita – American or Japanese -- you want or look at both and know some Akitas before you make this decision.

3. Make a list of reputable, ethical breeders who are known to have fine, stable animals.

Visit them and their dogs before you choose YOUR Akita. Ask those who know or check out the two Akita Clubs for breeder references. www.akitaclub.org and www.akita-inu.org Three clues to a good breeder are: how long the breeder has been in business, how often they show their dogs (even if you want your dog as a pet only), and definitely some buyer references. See Bonus Section: Questions you should ask any breeder.

4. Consider the negatives and the positives of Akitas and discuss them with your family, roommate, or whoever will be sharing the Akita with you. The Akita is a joy, a love, an affectionate very bright special dog with lots of responsibilities connected with ownership.

5. Plan on training dollars and time, and all the other expenses connected with an Akita. This is a big dog and has big expenses. If these expenses are daunting, you might be happier with another breed.

6. Akitas need inside homes, lots of attention, daily exercise, a very high fence for when you let him off leash outdoors, and patience in training.

If you can do these things to become an Akita owner, and you feel the Akita calling out to you, go for it!

CHAPTER 4:
Housing and Exercise for your Akita

Housing

Dog Crates or Dog Taxis as they are sometimes called

If your new Akita is put into a crate – or Dog Taxis as they are sometimes called -for housebreaking and you leave the door open while he is not in it, you will help him see that it is also a nice place to get a little peace and quiet.

I get it that most people think putting him in a crate is terrible, a kind of solitary confinement for dogs. But in truth, your dog's large crate is his best friend, not his worst.

When a puppy is put into a crate, its overhead ventilated "ceiling" and its closed- in sides are not threatening or frightening to your Akita; they are reassuring. This is his private cozy den.

Of course, if you use his crate as punishment, then that will influence how he considers his crate. If you extend his time in it long past when he needs to have food, or water, or exercise, or your company, or relieve himself, then he will change his perception of his nice warm cozy den.

But otherwise, from the get go, he will see it as HIS OWN CUBBY HOLE TO RETREAT TO WHEN HE IS TIRED OR NEEDS SOME QUIET TIME.

His crate will help you help him adjust to his new home. Set his crate near your bed at night – with him in it – and maybe an old shirt you've worn during that day. He will hear you breathe, smell your scent, and feel comforted by your presence.

You won't have to keep his crate there forever. He should adjust to his new home in a few days.

Otherwise, he may howl and cry all night and you will be gritting your teeth, and getting angrier and angrier. That has you both starting off on the wrong paws.

Even dogs with separation anxiety problems benefit from this technique. I once had a dog who did suffer from this common dog malady and I turned in desperation to a dog behavior specialist.

He displayed his separation anxiety attacks by chewing every textile I owned, and worse eating the torn up fabric bits. This is an emergency surgical procedure in the offing.

Advised to put his crate –which he hadn't had to use in a long time – by my bedside, I cheerfully did so and in a few nights, he was cured of his chewing. And I was a much happier camper.

I was also advised to refrain from paying any attention to him for a half hour before leaving the house, and another half hour upon my return. It seems that dogs get anxious when they have no time to adjust before your departures and returns.

Another way to house your new Akita is to create a nest for him in a large open wire mesh cage with an old blanket or thick padding. Even when he can see out, he still feels comforted by its overhead "ceiling" and sides. The larger open crate can be used after he's housebroken.

NO Outdoor Dog Houses for this breed

The most important thing to know about an Akita is they are an Inside the House kind of dog.

They will not be happy and your relationship will not get off the ground if you put him in a doghouse in the back yard. An Akita requires lots and lots of attention and your Akita NEEDS IT from YOU.

Exercise

How much does he need?

An Akita is accustomed to living inside with his family. As said earlier, he can even live in an apartment unlike some other large power breeds.

He can be relatively docile inside. But he NEEDS that 30 to 60 minute exercise routine daily. Some energetic exercise during that time period will leave him feeling mellow and ready to be calmer.

If you can't or choose not to do this daily, please consider another dog. This is a necessity for an Akita.

You've no doubt heard that Akitas need a lot of attention. That's true. And the more attention and friendly handling they get from their loved ones, the better their temperament.

In addition to his 30 to 60 minutes to energetic outdoor play, you can add other kinds of exercise to his and your life.

Akitas love agility training so that's another
possibility when your dog is ready for it and can
work with other dogs near him.

Another way for you to exercise your dog is to travel
with him, go camping with him or just enjoy hikes in
the woods or on a deserted beach.

Carrying your camping equipment and/or pulling a
sled needs additional training but once you get the
basic skills down and your position as an Alpha Pack
Leader established, there are lots of ways your Akita
and you can get exercise together.

We'll be talking about how to acclimate him to ride
in a car without any problems in the Traveling with
Your Akita chapter.

Another simple way to give him some exercise (n
addition to his more strenuous exercise) is to teach
him some easy tricks that can be done with a large
dog. It's a great way to bond with him yet let him
know who the Alpha Pack Leader is in a pleasant
way.

There is a list of easy to teach tricks at the latter part

of this book. Not only are they great fun for you and your family and your Akita, but they help you reinforce the basic commands: Sit, Stay, Down, and Come.

Of course you teach him other commands as you work with him; there is no limit to what you can teach this very smart canine.

Just remember your three training rules: CLARITY, CONSISTENCY, AND PATIENCE.

CHAPTER 5:
Nutrition for your Akita

It may surprise you to learn that your very large Akita does not eat much. Wolves – his closest ancestors – took a fast day weekly to eat only fruits and berries. This helped prepare his digestive system for the week's meat eating diet.

The wolf normally ate once a day but when he did, he ate many parts of his prey, including those that provided him with digestive enzymes.

While you probably will not put your Akita puppy through this weekly spa–like internal cleansing, you can and should plan your Akita's diet to suit his breed.

That said, the first thing you will ask a breeder you have decided to buy your Akita from is "What do you feed the puppy and how often?"

This is information that you will use to continue that diet for a time after you bring your dog home, before gradually switching to the diet you will use to raise and nurture him.

Most dogs have their diets changed by first eating a mix of his old and new foods, then gradually getting less and less of his original foods and more and more of his new foods until he is switched. This normally takes a week or two, but the best way is to get explicit instructions from the breeder who raised your puppy.

Most large dogs are fed twice daily. Again, check with your breeder. You should always be able to call your breeder if you have a question. She knows your dog better than anyone.

Fresh food or dry kibble?

Some breeders have worked out fresh food diets for their Akitas. They are composed of fresh meats, vegetables, and even some dairy foods.

While some excellent breeders recommend high premium natural ingredient commercial foods, others swear by the BARF diet – Biologically Appropriate Raw Food.

This diet is high in protein, and includes cottage cheese, eggs, yogurt, vegetables and some leafy greens. Since dogs are frequently allergic to corn and soy, these ingredients are not included in this diet. BARF advocates also feed their dogs natural fresh bones.

BARF diet foods vary depending on the breeder. However, the basics remain the same. BARF advocates also say that premium kibble diets must have "raw foods" incorporated in them to maintain a balanced diet for your dog.

Historically, Akitas in Japan ate fish, rice, seaweed and vegetables. Because this exact diet unlikely to be easily duplicated in your community, it's recommended that your Akita takes a digestive enzyme tablet daily along with his meals.

You can get these (human) dietary enzyme caplets at your local health food store. They should include oxbile, pancratin, pepsin, rodelaine, betaine and papain.

Other supplements the Akita needs are kelp and a daily multivitamin. It's been said that human vitamins and enzymes are better than those created specifically for dogs. Since the human ones are less expensive, that makes two reasons to use the human variety. In fact, perfectly good multivitamins can be bought for next to nothing at variety or "box" stores.

Whether you feed your dog fresh foods or dry "kibble", the majority of protein for an Akita must come from chicken, turkey, fish or meat. Never beef or horsemeat.

Whichever diet you decide upon for your dog, it must contain high quality, easy to digest protein. **It must be an all natural food with no soy products.**

Between 24-26 percent should be protein while fat should be limited to 16 percent.

Less protein and fat are required for older dogs. There are special formulas created for your older animal companion.

Check labels not only for percentages *but also the source of the protein*. "Chicken byproducts" can be the ground up beaks and feet of chicken – a far cry from that nice juicy chicken or turkey leg you may be imagining for your Akita.

Dry "kibble", which incidentally helps decrease your dog's teeth's tartar, a "biggie' when it comes to your dog's overall health, should be the highest quality premium natural foods you can buy and contain NO additives, preservatives or artificial colors.

Natural preservatives like Vitamin C and E are used in premium all natural foods. Check out some of the all natural dog foods in your local health food or natural foods store. Natural foods can help extend the length of your dog's life.

Look for a printed label or logo and note on the packaging that says their foods have passed the American Association of Feed Control Officials feeding trials. That means you can trust that product to have the right ingredients for your puppy, young or adult dog.

Many dog owners rely on generic dog foods in the mistaken belief that the extra money is not worth it – that dog food is dog food. No, it won't immediately kill your dog to eat this "doggie junk food", but as he gets older, the results of a poor diet will begin to show.

The few extra dollars for premium natural food for your Akita as a puppy and as an adult will pay off in the end in a healthy dog and fewer vet bills.

Incidentally, if AAFCO Feeding Trial label is not printed on the package, call the manufacturer and ask them if it has passed the feeding trials and if so, is that so for your Akita?

If their number is not on the box, and not in your 1-800 directory, ask the manager of the store where their product is sold for the company's customer service number. Ten to ten he has it in his files.

Wet canned food versus dry dog foods

BARF diets and dry dog foods are not your only two choices when it comes to feeding your dog a balanced meal. There is also canned (wet) food and semi moist foods.

Some recommend that puppies have their dry food put down and left there all day, then have a half can of food mixed with dry twice a day.

If you can't free feed your dog for some reason during the day, or choose not to leave his food out all day, feed puppies three times a day.

The happy news is that any good breeder will send you off not only with your Akita, but the food your Akita needs to start his life with you and a complete packet of information including a detailed diet.

An adult Akita diet

If you have had your Akita since he was a puppy, you have no doubt already created a healthy diet for him.

However, if you are getting an adult dog and you have not been advised what the dog needs to thrive, here is one feeding suggestion offered by an Akita rescue group.

"Akitas may be prone to skin diseases if fed the wrong food. The Akita needs an all natural, Premium food with high quality easily digested protein. . . Feed stores and pet stores carry dry kibble, which are suitable for feeding Akitas," sys the Akita rescue group.

"First soak the dry food, the add a half-can of Mighty Dog, half a can of Kal-Kan canned food or Campbell's soup, mixed with at least a half cup of warm water."

They, like other Akita experts, recommend that digestive enzymes and a multivitamin/mineral be added to their food.

You need to check the label for the product's ingredients. On dog food labels as with labels of food for humans, the order of ingredients on the label tells you how much of it is in that food. If the first item is corn, then corn is the major ingredient in the product. And on down the ingredient list.

Feeding an adult Akita by free choice is not recommended. Instead, put his food down for his feeding, then pick it up. A normal feeding schedule for a full grown Akita is twice a day although under certain conditions, once daily may be better for your Akita. *See the Health chapter in this book.*

TREATS

Most experts recommend that treats be limited to 10 percent of your dog's diet. No table foods should be fed to dogs, even as a treat.

If you feed your dog bones, you should always supervise him while he is chewing them. They can splinter or break and your dog may need help if they do.

Since dogs like all kinds of treats, you can offer a variety of doggie treats to your Akita. You'll quickly learn which of them his favorites are.

There are hard baked cookies, huge smoked bones, those faux bones created with a potato base (often good for dogs with food intolerances) I've already mentioned, and the usual rawhide twists and bones and rope bones.

There are also treats made now that are hypo-allergenic with natural ingredients and no artificial color or preservatives that could be harmful to your dog. A well known movie star manufactures some very healthy allergen free treats.

You will also see slick looking pretty colored bones called Velvets on the market.

Some folks believe they should never be fed to your Akita. They contain corn starch; if he has food allergies or food intolerances, corn may be one trigger. Dogs are frequently allergic to wheat and corn. On the other hand, YOUR dog may do well with them. Try anything new in small offerings. Then observe your dog for a couple of hours. Any diarrhea or vomiting can be attributed to the new treat.

A number of vets have also warned about rawhide chew items ... whether sticks or "bones" or even huge sturdy looking twists.

Yes, I know that some are labeled "Approved by vets"

but many vets say that anything rawhide is dangerous to a puppy or dog.

A dog may swallow pieces of the rawhide, and that if he does so, it can and has caused obstructions in a dog's intestines, necessitating surgery to remove it.

Other vets recommend rawhide treats only when supervised. For the same reason.

I have always taken their advice even though my dog Wolf loved rawhide the one time he ever had any!

He's learned to love the huge edible "bones" made of potato and turkey and rice instead. He chews just as hard on this as on rawhide and I am a much calmer guy.

Again, your pet is unique and his treats need to fit his desires so choose them by the "try and see" method. As with his meal diet, natural treats without additives and artificial colors are recommended.

WATER

Akitas are big animals and need a lot of water to

remain hydrated throughout the day.

That said, a great helper is the large automatic watering container you can buy just about anywhere now. The water keeps coming all day; it stays clean and it's easily refilled. Check out your local pet supply store or a pet supply catalog.

Two good suggestions for outdoor water provision come from an animal cruelty officer who all too often sees the results of accidental and non accidental dehydration in dogs.

Any time your Akita is in the yard, he should have some way to get fresh water. In warm weather, he needs to have even more access to cool clean water.

One suggestion is to put two large bowls of water out so if he spills one, he will still have water.

Another suggestion is to buy a large metal bucket with a handle, and attach it to a fence or tree so your dog cannot easily spill it. Of course, he may wash himself in it and you will have to refill it but a hose can clean it out and easily refill it.

Water for your Akita should be de-chlorinated. Check with your town or city if you get your water from a central source. They can provide you with a free water supply analysis. You'd be surprised at what's in some water sources.

Buying a water filtering system for your faucet is a good investment for you and your dogs. They are not expensive. Check out what the filters cost; sometimes the filters cost more than the system you screw onto your faucet. Shop around. Big Do-It-Yourself stores are your best places to find a good inexpensive system and filters.

CHAPTER 6:
Identification for your Akita

While all dogs should wear a collar with identification noting his name, telephone number and owner (It can't hurt to also add REWARD in big letters), collars can fall off. They can be taken off. Wrong addresses and telephone numbers may accidentally stay on them after you've moved. You can find yourself in a natural disaster and you may be separated from your animal companion.

It is strongly advised that all dogs be micro-chipped.

Micro chipping is easy, it's quick, it's inexpensive -- and it's forever.

What is micro chipping?

A pet identification microchip is a tiny rice grain-sized micro chip, similar to those in computers, which is inserted under the pet's skin. It never moves, and it's permanent.

It isn't activated until you enroll your pet in the database program that acts as a central information base.

You can get inexpensive micro-chipping through your local humane society or ASPCA, or from your vet. Price vary depending on where you are located

Let me tell you the heartwarming story of Dudley Do-Good.

Dudley Do-Good, a male English bulldog, was stolen from Mr. Hoby Urich of Aubrey, Texas, after he had owned him for only two days. He was taken from Mr. Urich's porch.

What the thief didn't know was that Dudley Do-Good had a microchip imbedded between his shoulder blades.

Almost a year later, a Good Samaritan found the dog wandering the streets in Dallas, miles from home. He took Dudley to the Society for the Prevention of Cruelty to Animals' facility. Dudley was scanned and lo and behold, there was the chip. The two friends were quickly reunited.

How does a Microchip work?

It's really so simple that it's no surprise someone came up with it.

The chip has a numerical code on it. Once it's imbedded, the chip can be "read" with special equipment – which is pretty widely owned by animal groups and many vets these days.

The American Kennel Club has a database on the animals.

The official name for the pet microchip is The HomeAgain Companion Animal Retrieval System and it's produced by Schering-Plough Animal Health Corp.

Once you have your dog micro-chipped, you pay about $15.00 to the microchip's manufacturer's database and you're in business.

"It's a passive device, meaning that the transponder carries no battery and remains inactive except when it is being scanned," the company's Website reports.

You may never be in a disaster like Hurricanes Francis, Ivan or Jeannie, or the incredible catastrophe of Hurricane Katrina, but if you are and your pet survives, and he is micro-chipped, *you will be reunited.*

What do you know about Pet Insurance?

This is also a good time to consider getting health insurance for your dog.
With the high cost of veterinary and animal hospital care, it is a boon that there are companies that specialize in insuring your pet.

At the recommendation of my vet, I bought health insurance for my dog when he was several months old. As I recall, it cost less than a cheap dinner out and it only costs that once a month.

Three days later, I walked into the living room – It was Thanksgiving Day -- and my guy sat there with red all over his mouth and tongue and teeth. No, fortunately, he was not bleeding – he had eaten my friend's lipstick, tube and all!

My first emotion was terror. My second, after learning I had to take him to an Emergency Vet who charged me an extra hefty fee for holiday exams, was horror – of a different kind.

The vet gave him excellent treatment – and I gave him the down payment for new SUV hubcaps.

My next emotion was – Hurrah, I have insurance for this!

I've used this pet insurance several times. It recently cost me over two hundred dollars to get my dog's teeth cleaned. That's more than one year's premiums.

Let's put it his way: I bought Wolf's insurance policy so that I never have to say, "I can't afford that treatment."

I may drop my health insurance but never Wolf's.

Check online. There are several excellent pet insurance companies out there.   Each has different deductible schedules and benefit payments. Compare their literature and choose which is best for you and Suki.

CHAPTER 7:
Grooming your Akita

Because Akitas have double coats, the outer one coarse, upstanding and a little longer (called the guard coat), and the undercoat lush and thick and soft, they have unique grooming needs.

Normally, Akitas have moderate grooming needs. They usually need to have a complete grooming – bathing and nail care – about every six to eight weeks.

But twice or three times annually, they shed such volumes of hair; it is called "blowing" their coats. This takes some serious daily brushings and attention.

Check the Brushing segment below for some groomers' advice on how you can handle this hurricane of hair.

Otherwise, a weekly mini grooming includes brushing him, clipping his paw hair even with his pads, brushing his teeth, and cleaning his ears and eyes. His nail care may or may not be part of this mini-grooming.

When you go into his ears, do not go deep in them; a vet needs to clean the canals inside his ears. Just wipe the upper outside part of his ears. *More about his ears and eyes and teeth in the Health chapter.*

During bathing, always put wads of cotton in his ears before you use any water on him. Don't forget to take the cotton wads out after his bath.

All dogs love the way they feel after they are groomed. Your Akita will, too.

Bathing your Akita

This section incorporates the advice of a number of groomers. I want you to have the input of different professionals who have dealt with an Akita in the tub and in the drying process. Just realize that however you bathe him, it will take time. Some professionals suggest you allow a day for bathing your big friend!

Hands on Bath Time

Supplies to have on hand include a bathing basin of some sort or a bathtub, mild *tearless* puppy or adult dog shampoo, a shower hose that can be attached to your faucet, all your brushing tools, cotton wads for his ears, and lots of towels. You also need a hair dryer made specifically for a dog; human hair dryers get too hot and may burn your dog's skin.

Consider asking for a little help from another member of the family or another Akita owner. This is a two-person job if you need to lift him out of the tub. (You might offer to swap bathing help.)

You can also bathe him in a large shower stall. Whether you use a shower or a bathtub, always have a non slip rubber bath mat for him to stand or sit on. And if you value your plumbing, you need to get a stopper that catches all that loose hair.

Of course, if it's hot summer, you have a high fence, a gate that can be locked, a child's swimming pool and a garden hose, you have a perfect dog-spa bathing situation.

Just be sure to bring him in the house to dry off before the sun goes down and it's getting cooler outside. First, allow him to shake a lot of the water off himself. He will definitely enjoy that. Then dry him off with his dog hair dryer inside. Most dogs like this attention and slight warmth on them. It's a warm air massage.

Above all, do not use dish detergent or human shampoo on your Akita. They dry your dog's skin and hair.

Dog hair in general is very different from human hair. The Akita's coat is water resistant and weather resistant; you will not want to remove that natural coating by using the wrong shampoo or washing him too often. Most groomers recommend washing a dog only every month or so to avoid drying out the dog's skin.

Ready to Wash

Suggestions are different for his bathing depending on his shedding season. Let's look first at the bathing you give him when he is not shedding.

First, brush your Akita well. Start with a slicker brush or steel pin brush to remove any loose hair. Then follow that by combing him out with a huge coarse comb. Misting him with water before you brush him (You can buy a misting bottle in your local discount store.) will keep his hair from blowing all over the room and YOU.

Be patient with him; this may not be fun for you but that may go double for your Akita, who has to stand through it all.

NEVER use hot water to wash your dog. You could scald him.
Always use lukewarm water instead.

Here's how to tell if the water temperature is "lukewarm."

Turn on the water, regulate both faucets, and then test the water's temperature by splashing a little on the inside of your arm. If the water feels lukewarm to you, it will to your dog.

Never wet your Akita's head first. It will upset him and the experience will start off badly. Always start at his withers. Wet him down, apply shampoo that has been diluted and start massaging it into a lather. Talk to your dog while you wash him and reassure him that this is nice.

Move slowly up his body towards his head. Wash the back o f his head carefully so that you do not get water or soap on his face. You can hold your hand like a guard on the top of his head to control the shampoo and water.

Note: Bathing him gives you a good chance to check out his health condition. Take a look at his skin for flakiness or rashes. He might be allergic or have food intolerances. Feel for lumps or bumps. He could have a cyst. Check for fleas. Observe *any* differences in his body. Smell him. Do you scent any foul odors? If you find any of these things, contact your vet.

Then, just before you end the bath, you can use a soft cloth to wash his face.

Now it's time to use that spray hose. Spray him until every bit of shampoo has been washed off. If you leave any shampoo on him, it will dry his skin, and it will make him itch.

Never spray him in the face.

Always use tearless mild dog shampoo.

Note: There are specialty shampoos made for flea control, specific color dogs and for dogs who are itching from allergies. Check them out at your local pet supply store or ask your groomer what she recommends. She can tell you what she uses for these Akita special bathing needs.

Towel dry him and let him shake off a lot of water. He will really enjoy that so let him shake until he seems done. Plan ahead for this part. Where can he shake off lots and lots of water during cooler months? Summers, he has the great outdoors.

Finish his drying with his dog hair dryer. Again, don't be tempted to use a human hair dryer. It's too hot for his skin and his hair.

Move his hair dryer slowly back and forth about a foot and a half or more from his body until his two coats, outer and under, are dry. This will take a long time. Don't be surprised if he falls asleep.

Grooming during his "Blow" times

It's recommended that during his mega-shedding or "Blow" times, he be washed once weekly and brushed every day. The goal is to remove and keep removing all his loose hair, of which there will seem to be a seemingly endless supply.

You can bathe and groom your Akita yourself although during the two or three times a year that he "blows" his coat, he sheds so much hair, it can cover a small room's floor. During these times, you might want help. You can eliminate the chore by handing it over to a professional groomer.

This breed-specific mega-shedding is normal so you might as well accept that it IS going to happen.

But it's only two or three times at most a year. Some large, long-haired dogs are known to shed all the time!

Brushing his Hair – During his Blow Times

If it's not summer and the weather is not too warm, you can help keep the hair from spreading throughout your house by putting a t-shirt on your dog.

Then, in the evenings, you can brush his undercoat with an under rake grooming tool, then a metal in brush and then a softer bristle brush. You can get any of the tools you need at a pet supply store or a good pet supply catalog. And online.

It's advised that you rake his undercoat, which removes all the loose hairs, outside on a flat, easily cleaned surface like your porch. Or perhaps you might lay a painter's drop cloth on the ground and sit him on it while you brush and brush.

Hers' some great news: The more he is groomed, the faster the shedding will end.

As for all that hair, would you believe there are actually productive uses for it?

Dog hair is useful in compost heaps; after all, it's pure nitrogen.

And, this may sound rather weird, but some owners

gather up their dog's hair "blow", twist it into yarn-like threads and knit sweaters and hats out of it!

One gal I know has a ball of this kind of hair on her home office desk that she keeps adding to each time her dog does its shedding thing. She says she's planning a sweater of her dog's hair for sentimental reasons.
These sweaters and hats are very soft, very warm and long wearing.

Professional knitters buy this dog hair from long haired dog owners. It seems that there is a great demand for these sweaters. Who woulda thought!

Grooming your Akita's Nails

Keeping your dog's nails clipped short is something he may do most of if he runs on hard or rough surfaces. However, this doesn't always happen.

If you ever see a large dog like an Akita whose nails have been badly neglected, you will know it. An Akita's nails may grow so long, they turn back towards the dog's compact "cat's paws" and deform the dog's paws. Or, worse, they are curved so far back that the dog is actually walking on his own nails!

I saw this once and I saw how the dog walked; all its

leg and hip joints were out of balance and his gait was badly affected. With any dog, this is disastrous but with an Akita, whose breed's tendency to hip problems is well known, it is life threatening.

So even if the dog is not yet ready to have a complete grooming, you need to watch its nails and clip them or have them clipped short *as needed*.

When is it needed? You'll hear a clicking sound when he walks on a hard surface.

Clipping an Akita's nails is not a walk in the park if he doesn't like it so it's suggested you start doing it when he is a puppy. Like touching his ears, the earlier you start, the more he will believe it's normal everyday behavior.

Even so, it's best if you have someone hold his paw steady while you clip his nails.
And move slowly. Trim a tiny bit at a time. And have a septic stick on hand to stop bleeding in case you accidentally cut into his nail vein.

Some dogs' nails are white or light colored and it's easy to see where the black looking vein ends. It could help to shine a flashlight on them or do this in bright sunlight. Other dogs' nails may be dark or even black and then you have to rely on your sense of touch not to take off too much and accidentally cut into his vein.

Again, move slowly. Clip a **tiny** bit off the hard pointed edge of his nail. Then feel the entire nail. How far are you from the part that feels softer? If you are still quite a ways from the hard part (that's where the vein is located), you can clip a tiny bit more. Better less than more.

Note: My groomer recommends cutting dog's nails just a little bit at a time, but often, like once weekly. This way, the nails' veins will slowly recede and be less likely to be cut into by mistake.

If this is your first Akita – it should never be your first dog – and you feel a little intimidated by this chore, you can benefit from tutoring in this procedure.

A vet can show you how to clip your dog's nails. There are several kinds of nail clippers you can use to clip your Akita's nails that are widely available. You want one that will easily and quickly cut tough nails.

An alternative is to ask your breeder to show you how she does this and watch carefully. Ask her what kind of clippers she uses.

I'm normally all thumbs -- so I opt for letting my groomer take care of my dog's nails. I've also had my vet's technician cut his nails during regular exams. Most groomers charge a nominal fee – or nothing – to clip your dog's nails if he is a regular client.

Note: As your dog gets older, his nails will need more attention.

CHAPTER 8:
Your Akita's Health

The most important thing you must do after bringing your new Akita home is to take him to his first visit to his veterinarian. If you don't yet have a vet and the breeder has no recommendation, (if you live far from your breeder, he may or may not know a vet in your location), check with your local ASPCA or Humane Society. They often work with excellent veterinarians and animal hospitals.

All new puppies need a baseline complete physical exam even if his pedigree papers include his inoculations, heartworm and other preventives listed.

A baseline exam, the first one, should be done from between 48 and 72 hours after you get him home. Your vet will do a complete physical exam on your dog; he will want to do a fecal test for parasites if you haven't brought him some fresh stool (in a plastic zip-lock bag) and he may want to do a blood test for giardiasis, a protozoan that can cause your dog to have chronic stomache upsets.

Your vet will also give your dog any immunizations he has not had, although all his early immunizations will have likely – but not necessarily -- been done by the breeder.

If your dog is 7 weeks or older, he should have had a Bordetella injection to protect him from kennel cough, a highly contagious disease.

Your vet can tell you if your dog already has a disease. Then you can make a decision how you want to respond to that.

If he has worms, you may decide to have him treated and keep him.

If he has distemper, a fatal disease, you may want to contact your breeder immediately. Will he return your money? Will he replace your dog? What was the original agreement should health problems exist?

However, right now, take a vow not to "borrow trouble". Your dog is very unlikely to have any medical problems, and if so, they will be most likely be fleas, worms or missing an immunization of two. These things can be taken care of on the spot by your dog's best friend, his new vet.

This is the time to ask all the questions you have of

the vet. Take a list with you so that you won't forget any of them. A good vet will be happy to answer them all; educating YOU is part of his job!

The Akita's Genetically Related Diseases

The Akita is prone to some diseases more than others. That does not mean he will definitely get them. It only means that keeping an eye out for any telling symptoms so that you can get him prompt treatment is necessary.

The most common Akita breed specific diseases are: Bloat (Gastric Dilatation and Volvulus), HipDysplasia, Hypothyroidism, Progressive Retinal Atrophy, Panepidermal pustular pemphigus (also known as pemphigus erythematosus), Sebaceous Adenitis, (PF), and VKH, or Vogt Koyanagi Harada Syndrome.

A list of those diseases, their symptoms, treatment modes, and some preventative measures follows:

Bloat or gastric dilatation-volvulus (GDV)

Bloat is life threatening. It can kill your dog within an hour. If you suspect it, take him immediately to his vet.

In bloat, the dog's stomach fills with air, food, and/or water, then swells and twists until it seals off the openings from which air can be expelled. This swollen stomach squeezes the heart, nerves and blood supply. Without immediate medical care, it will result in a swift death.

Symptoms: Swollen belly, "dry" vomiting, restlessness, pain in his abdomen when you touch it, rapid shallow breathing, crying, a lot of drooling or salivating, and collapse.

Treatments needed immediately: Stomache pumped to express air; surgery.

Preventative measures: Feed your dog small meals two to three times a day; take up his water for an hour or so after meals but make water available to him the rest of the time. It's better to put down smaller amounts of water consistently than large amounts at once. He may gulp down too much at once. Try to keep him calm and unstressed and not overly stimulated for an hour before eating and two hours after eating. Do not exercise him heavily right after he eats.

Note: All cases of bloat must have surgical attention, even if after the air is expressed. His stomache must be stitched back into the correct place or the torsion will simply happen again. Perhaps as soon as hours later. Studies report that 85 percent of dogs who have not had follow-up surgery die.

Please see "Does your dog need health insurance?" With pet health insurance in place, cost will not be the same consideration. Ask your employee if your company insurance includes this option. Lots of companies are now aware of how pets are family members and do offer pet insurance.

Hip Dysplasia

Akitas are unfortunately prone to hip dysplasia. This happens when the head of the femur bone, which normally fits into the hip joint like the ball in a socket, cannot do this because the hip joint is too shallow or the edges too worn down by the disease to hold the femoral head properly.

If you would like to feel what that means, stand up, put your fingertips on your "hip bones" and wiggle your hips. You should be able to feel how your hips' femurs' heads rock in their sockets.

103

Very time the dog moves that joint, the femur "ball" moves out of the socket a bit. Eventually, the dog develops what's called osteo (bone) arthritis. Since this is a progressive disease, arthritis gets worse with time.

To ensure that their litters are not affected by hip dysplasia, ethical breeders submit x-rays of their breeders to the Orthopedic Foundation for Animals (or OFA).

There, the OFA's panel of American College of Veterinary Radiologists check the dogs' x-rays for any signs of this disease. The OFA then certifies the dogs according to the classifications designated by the three Radiologists: Excellent, good, fair, borderline, mildly dysplastic or severely dysplastic. Check your breeders' certification for dates as well as classifications. When was the last time the OFA certification was done on your Akita's parents?

Symptoms: Sometimes, in young dogs, there are no symptoms and the disease is only discovered when he is older and after x-ray scans are done.

Pain and lameness in the hips will alert you to your older dog's hip dysplasia. If your Akita starts to limp or act like he's having some pain in his hip or joints, you need to take him to his vet. He will need a series of x-rays with your dog placed in specific OFA-recommended positions. Your vet may need to anesthetize your dog to be able to do this.

Treatment varies: Since there is no cure for hip dysplasia, you need to help your dog manage his or her pain. This can mean pain medications and/or some acupuncture, which has been found to be helpful in pain management for canines.

Keep her weight down, work with the vet in her pain management plan, and exercise your Akita appropriately. That means playing with her in a way that will not required jarring of the joints. Walk instead of jog; having him chase a Frisbee or catch a ball is not a good idea now. Perhaps hide and seek (where you hide something and encourage your dog to find it) and similar games plus walking would be better for your Akita now.

You will need to watch out for your dog; did you ever see how a child will run and resist sleep until they drop, even when they are ill or even have a fever? Well, that's your Kedo or Suki. Both will obey you until he or she drops.

If the pain gets too severe for your dog, you may have to resort to hip replacement surgery.

Hypothyroidism

Medical explanation: Hypothyroidism is an underproduction of the hormone thyroxin. The thyroid gland and this hormone combine to influence the dog's development and growth.

Symptoms: There are a number of symptoms you can watch for; the main ones being loss of appetite, unusual and seemingly unwarranted aggression, hair loss, oily skin, itching and others. If he seems out of sorts and nothing seems to be justifying it, you may want to have your vet check his thyroid production.

Treatment: The happy news is that this condition is reversible. The usual treatment is an oral thyroid supplement. Your vet will give you the dosage and frequency when he prescribes the proper supplement.

Progressive Retinal Atrophy

Progressive retinal atroply is actually one of a group of diseases responsible for the gradual deterioration of canine's eyes' retinas. First the cells that control his night vision are lost; later the cone cells – those responsible for day vision are lost.

Symptoms: He may suddenly seem nervous about going out at night, perhaps like he's suddenly afraid of the dark. His eyes may suddenly shine more than you've noticed before. Your dog may develop cataracts.

Treatments: This is a gradual process that could take years although it can occur when the dog is young, or may develop as he gets older. Cataracts can be removed. Any change in the appearance of a cataract requires an immediate visit to your vet.

It is predicted that your dog will adjust quite well to being sightless as long as his environment and lifestyle remains the same. Sometimes, another pet will start to take over as a companion to your companion.

But he is still your Akita, a faithful friend who will continue to love and protect you. Akita's other senses are so keen that often their blindness is not immediately recognizable to others.

Panepidermal pustular pemphigus or Pemphigus Erythematosus and Pemphigus foliaceus

Pemphigus, as it's commonly referred to, is a complex of skin diseases caused by an impaired auto-immune system. Pemphigus erythematosus is a milder form of P. Foliaceus. The former usually affects the face and feet of the dog, while the latter can eventually affect the dog's entire body.

It is assumed that Akitas are genetically disposed to these two varieties of Pemphigus.

Symptoms: Blisters, scabs, crusts, and loss of pigmentation which may start at the bridge of the nose and then be seen around the eyes, ears, and as it develops into the more serious P. Foliaceus, it could affect his entire body.

Treatment: Your veterinarian will need to diagnosis this disease since its symptoms can imitate other diseases like systemic and discoid lupus, or cancer. A skin biopsy can determine the correct diagnosis.

And, as with a human diagnosis, a second opinion is always an option.

Sebacious Adenitis

If you've ever had a rash or fever sore and can't figure out why but it's uncomfortable anyway, you will empathize with your Akita if he suddenly shows symptoms of Sebacious Adenitis. It's not life threatening but it can precipitate bacterial infections.

And it's very unpleasant to have.

SA is an inflammation of the sebaceous glands; unfortunately, no one seems to know what causes it. There is some thought that it could be genetic but there's not even solid proof of that. It's not uncommon for Akitas to be afflicted with it.

Symptoms: Scaling that looks like dandruff that clings close to the hair's roots; it usually starts on the face and tips of his ears and there is hair loss – sometimes extensive hair loss.

Treatment: Your best good fortune will be to get an immediate correct diagnosis. SA can mask itself with symptoms that mirror allergies or other diseases. Even when correctly diagnosed, however, there is no cure. Antibiotics are prescribed for any secondary bacterial infections; your vet may prescribe medications for allergies; some owners have used herbal concoctions which may work for periods of time – or not work at all.

Your vet can recommend the latest medications and help you develop a maintenance comfort schedule of special shampoos and conditioners. If your Akita gets a bacterial infection, your vet can prescribe an antibiotic.

You may be more upset than your Akita with this unexpected turn of events. If you are showing you dog, you will not be able to compete. If you had been planning to breed this Akita, this affliction will make it highly undesirable.

As for your Akita, it doesn't seem to bother him much unless he gets a bacterial infection which could increase his itching. This, too, however, can be dealt with at home.

For a poignant diary written by one Akita owner who worked through her Akita's SA with him, see www.akita-friends.com/special/SA/story.htm

VKH, or Vogt Koyanagi Harada Syndrome

The bonafide VHK is an autoimmune disease that normally affects people. Another version, also called VKH, or Vogt Koyanagi Harada Syndrome, afflicts dogs, and particularly Akitas. There is no medical information that connects the two syndromes at this time.

What is VKH? It's a deep inflammation of the eye tissues that leads to partial blindness. The process is called uveitis or uveodermatologic syndrome.

Strangely, in later stages, it turns the hair white – both in humans and canines.
It seems to be caused by the body's negative reaction

to its' own pigment-producing cells (melanocytes) although a virus is suspected.

Symptoms: Painful eyes, cloudy looking eyes; they may turn colors.

Treatments: A skin biopsy is needed to confirm the presence of the disease. Your dog's appearance can be affected by the skin's reaction to the disease. His eye disease is the focus of any treatment if blindness is to be avoided. You need to have your dog seen by a canine opthalmologist as well as your vet.

A referral to a canine specialist is not unusual today. Our animal companions are seeing not only animal behavioral psychologists, but being cared for by a retinue of specialists in special veterinary care centers.

In Dallas, Texas, a new concept in animal care started a trend that migrated across the country. The Veterinary Referral Center is located in one building wherein animal surgeons, pet neurologists, ophthalmologists, oncologists, dermatologists, radiologists and internal medicine specialists work to improve our pets' health.

Check your nearest large city; there may be a referral center there for your pet.

What else is new in pet health care?

There's laser surgery, new types of anesthesia, progressive radiological testing, DNA testing, pet massage therapy, acupuncture, animal behavioral psychologists, and the innovative care of holistic veterinarians – all now available to our animal companions with more "medicine of tomorrow" on its way.

Eye and Ear Care

Your Akita's Eyes

All dog's eyes need to be examined during routine physical exams. Older dog's eyes normally look a little cloudy but since that can also mean cataracts, glaucoma, or other eye diseases including PRA, be alert to changes in your Akita's eyes.

Some eye problems you may encounter with your Akita – at any age – are Progressive Retinal Atrophy, cataracts, glaucoma, conjunctivitis, and physical eye deformities.

If you are just buying your new Akita puppy, one way to determine your dog's freedom of eye diseases is to ask the breeder for the Akita's sire and dam's CERF (Canine Eye Registration Foundation) numbers.

Be observant of your Akita companion. If you see signs that his eyes are getting cloudy looking, changing color, shining more than usual, causing him pain, or he seems to be unusually afraid of the dark, or seems to be losing sight, take your dog to a canine opthalmologist. Ask your vet for a referral to this specialist.

Take your dog to a vet immediately if you see any of the above signs. Glaucoma – which is very painful -- can cause blindness within weeks or months – or even in just days. Surgery could relieve the fluid pressure in his eye or eyes, thereby saving his eyesight.

Note: Pet insurance will cover these visits and any necessary surgery if you have had his policy prior to the condition. Some carriers pay 80 percent of claims after a small deductible. If I sound pro-pet insurance, I am. It helps me give my dog the best health care possible and I am just a working guy who's been able to keep rotating vet dollars with my insurance claim refunds.

Dogs love you fussing over them. Adding a cleaning around their eyes to their weekly home mini-grooming keeps crud out of them, and decreases the change of bacteria getting a stranglehold on his eyelashes or hair around his eyes.

Cleaning around his eyes can be done with a soft non-fuzzy cloth, like a soft human face washing cloth, and warm water. (Test for lukewarm) Hold it wadded up so its corners will never accidentally scratch his eyes, and gently wipe off anything around his eyes.

A second way to clean around your dog's eyes is to use professional eye cleaning disposable pads available at any pet supply store. They have a base of sterile water UV and contain vet approved soothing ingredients. Unless you're going to machine wash cloths in hot water between each use, disposable pads are safer.

Ears

Akitas are prone to ear infections. Some of the most common ear problems for Akitas include Otitis Externa (outer ear infection), Otitis Media (middle ear infection) or damage to the inner ear like a broken eardrum. Since Akitas are quick to get ear mites, an ear mite infestation can also cause serious infections in your dog's ears.

Symptoms: Some of his symptoms can signal more than one ear problem; that is why it's very important to take him to his vet if he shakes his head a lot, refuses to eat, has painful ears, has bad smells coming from his ears, or he vomits. Any one of these symptoms, or a cluster of several, can alert the vet to further investigation and proper diagnosis. This is not time for a do it yourself approach.

Otitis Externa can be caused by a number of things including mites or fleas, allergies, diseases like SA or Pemphigus foliaceous (discussed earlier). He also could have got something in his ear accidentally, like a broken twig or some dirt or something else he had a great time rolling around in.

Treatments: Your vet will examine, x-ray and probably take specimens of the substance in your dog's ear(s). He will use an otoscope to look deep into the ear canal. He will examine your dog's ears inside and out, and check to see if the dog's eardrum is perforated.

He will prescribe the proper medication for your dog's particular problem. Watch as he cleans your dog's outer ears (Do not go deeper into your dog's ears. I know I've said this before but it's true. Your good intentions could injure his ear more if you dig inside the ear canal. This is reserved for your vet only.) However, you can learn from him how to clean the outer ear and how to insert drops in your dog's ears.

If your dog is suffering from an infection or other damage to an inner ear, he may need surgery to retain his hearing.

If your dog shows any of the symptoms outlined above, take him to his vet immediately.

Teeth and Gum Care

One thing is sure. All dogs must chew. They need to chew; they want to chew; they will chew. What your Akita will chew may amaze you.

They will chew anything they can get their mouths on and somehow they seem to know which are the expensive Spanish shoes or the special silk fringe on the new rug or even your movie star jazzy eyeglasses. In fact, if the frames are made of plastic, they will *especially* like to chew your glasses. All young dogs LOVE plastics but your great big Akita will chew your glasses AND your grandmother's antique rocking chair!

So, don't fight it, join it. Get your puppy or chew-happy adult dog something good to chew on.

There are a variety of chew-toys that not only satisfy your dog's urge to munch but also help to clean his teeth. And they come in sizes that can grow from puppy size to gigantic for super-chewers like your adult Akita.

One highly recommended one is made of heavy strong polyurethane. Some of these "bones" have protruding services that help scrape the tartar off the dog's teeth as he chews. They have a dog-delicious scent of food impregnated in them so your dog doesn't get bored with them.

Many chew toys are made of rawhide. Most vets do not recommend them in spite of their popularity and packages stamped with "Approved by vets." (I always wish the label told me which vets.)

Dogs can eat pieces of rawhide and choke. They can eat pieces that land up blocking their intestines. Yes, surgery has been needed in some cases to remove rawhide pieces. So some vets recommend alternatives.

These days, there are some good chew toys that are not rawhide. Nylabones® come in super sizes for the large dog; and rope toys – as long they are not the string kind which are appetizers for some "fiber happy" dogs -- are good alternative chew toys and dental care.

There is also super size, smoked real bones on the market. Yes, he will love them but if you decide to give them to your dog, please supervise when he has them and set them aside when you can't. Any bones can shatter and injure your dog.

There is also what are called Greenies® now on the market and dogs LOVE their taste. They love them so much they will eat this entire edible "bone" – no matter which size -- in nothing flat. If your dog tolerates the Greenie and it doesn't make him nauseous, fine, but a once a week Greenie® should be tops for your dog.

Cleaning your dog's teeth

As your dog gets older, and his adult teeth come in, he will get tartar on them – just as humans do.

Yes, you can brush your dog's teeth. And the sooner you start the better for you and your handsome/beautiful Akita.

In fact, the earlier you start examining your puppy's mouth, the more you will protect his oral health while teaching him to tolerate a vet's handling of his mouth and teeth and gums.

When plaque gets so heavy on your dog's teeth that it

affects his gums, he will have to be anesthetized by your vet so that his teeth can be scraped and have any periodontal deep cleaning done.

It's much easier to include a weekly teeth cleaning as part of his weekly mini-grooming. A regular kit containing puppy or dog rubber cleaning finger tip and toothbrush with dog-delicious toothpaste can be bought at any pet supply store for a nominal cost. We use Chicken flavor but there are others.

Some dogs like this tooth brushing (or finger brushing); others would rather not, thank you. He can't be forced to participate but he might be able to be bribed, or as some more sophisticated dog owners might say, "lured".

If he really likes the taste of his toothpaste but won't allow a toothbrush in his mouth, you can substitute a finger cleaning tip and a little taste of the toothpaste as a "lure."

Put the fingertip cleaning tool on the forefinger of your dominant hand; put some chicken (or beef) flavored doggie toothpaste on it, let him take a few licks, then wrap your arms around him. Speaking softly to him, gently brush first one side of his mouth's teeth, then the other with your rubber finger.

You will find your own way with your special Akita.

You and only you know what he will tolerate and how to approach him in a way that teeth cleaning can become a low problem grooming task.

However it gets done, it's worth the effort and then some.

Anesthetizing him – for whatever reason – is not inexpensive and older dogs or dogs with a health problem are more at risk for anesthesia-related complications.

Spaying and Neutering your Akita

Unless you are planning to breed your Akita, it is wise to spay her or neuter your Akita while he or she is very young; at the seventh or eighth month for a female; by the fifth month for a male dog.

Three advantages of spaying a bitch are: It eliminates in-heat behavior and messes, keeps male dogs from prowling and howling around your house, and eliminates that "in heat" scent that has male dogs trying to be "friendlier than friendly" when you walk her.

These are social reasons. The medical reasons for spaying (ovariohysterectomy) are far more compelling. Spaying her while young decreases her chances of getting mammary Cancer later to about 1 percent. That percent increases to about 8 if she is spayed before the second heat period. After that, her chances of getting mammary tumors increases to 25 percent, spayed or not.

Spaying also protects your bitch from uterus infections, called pyometra. The problem with this disease is that it can be present without any warning symptoms. A Pyometra-related infection, which requires expensive treatment, can become life threatening before you recognize if for what it is.

Bottom line is spaying helps your loving and loved bitch live longer.

Neutering

I've heard so many people say "Oh I would never do that to my dog." This happens most with folks who "humanize" their dogs. Neutering will not change him radically. It will make his and your life easier. It will not affect his personality. And he won't rise up in the night and say, "What have you done to me?" Believe it or not, neutering your Akita will make his and your life more pleasant.

Some of his breed-related aggressiveness will be decreased by early neutering, but it's your training and his environment that will mold his personality and temperament.

A medical reason for neutering your male Akita --

called performing an orchiectomy—is that it decreases the risk of him getting prostate problems as he gets older.

Neutering also keeps your dog at home and releases him from the constant physical need to keep chasing after bitches in heat.

For the record, my male dog is neutered and seems as happy to meet and court female dogs as ever. He just doesn't have to run away from home to do it.

While it is true that spayed bitches may become a little more aggressive and both genders may gain a little weight, these weight increases are not grossly abnormal.

Traditional surgery vs. laser surgery

Ask your vet if he offers the choice of laser surgery for spaying or neutering your animal.

There is a great difference in how the surgery is performed, how the animal responds to the surgery and how long it takes him to recuperate.

Laser surgery causes less pain, less bleeding, less swelling and more accurate surgery. Because there is less post-operative pain, your dog's recuperation can be counted in hours instead of days.

The cost is minimally more than traditional surgery. An hour after the surgery, my dog was bounding into my arms with no seeming distress except his annoyance at the need to temporarily wear an Elizabethan collar.

There are some legitimate concerns associated with the surgical and anesthesia-related risks involved with any surgical or dental cleaning procedure. Medical studies report that about one in every five hundred canines who undergo anesthesia die because of it.

When I heard that my dog could be at risk, depending on the anesthesia used, I began to research the kinds of anesthesia being used today.

Is one kind of anesthesia safer for your Akita than another?

The answer is yes.

There are two types of anesthesia used today to sedate animals: The injectant ones, the inhalant ones – and most times, a combination of both.

Vets I interviewed in two states told me the same thing: An injectable, or induction anesthetic, is not as easy to control as an inhalant.

As one veterinary hospital representative said, "If anything goes wrong while the dog is "under", a gas is reversible and can be quickly flushed out of the animal's body with oxygen."

Most times, an induction agent is used prior to giving the animal an inhalant, a gas called either sevoflurane or isofluorane. Both of these are relatively new inhalants that animals respond to well.

There should be on site equipment that will monitor your dog's vital signs and blood oxygen, just as yours would be monitored in a hospital. Most vets will require that your dog have pre-surgery blood tests to check his kidney and liver functions. If he doesn't mention them, you might ask to have them done. The cost is minimal and the information gained for your vet and you is invaluable.

One very frank vet advised not to accept the use of an injectable alone. She said they were simply not as controllable -- and impossible to reverse.

Note: Generally, unless your dog is older than five years old or has a health problem, there should be no complications due to anesthesia.

Protecting your Akita from Toxic Substances

Just as you would protect a toddler from poisonous household items by locking them away, so must your wonderful Akita be protected from his own curiosity and passion for new tastes.

For instance, did you know that drinking anti freeze/coolant leaking from your vehicle can kill your Akita?

Antifreeze/coolant looks like green water and most people don't pay attention to it as it pools under their vehicle.

Dogs love the sweet taste of antifreeze/coolant, and even a little can kill one.
Using propylene glycol instead of ethylene glycol is safer for your Akita.

Check out the command "Leave It" in this books' training section. It could save your dog's life.

Household cleaners, some over the counter medications, some bait traps, some plants, some foods, even some American coins, can injure or kill your Akita if he ingests them.

For a good household checklist you can use to prepare for your Akita's home safety BEFORE you bring him home, check out www.Petco.com/caresheets/dog/Dog_Household_D anger.Prf

Note: All animal owners should have the number of their local poison control center posted where they can easily see it or get it. Dogs and cats can come up with the most amazing things to eat. One large dog, reports one vet, ate a large kitchen knife. He survived with emergency surgical removal.

First Aid Kit for your Akita

Just as most households have a first aid kit or its equivalent for humans in their medical chests, a dog needs to have his first aid kit. One that travels in a metal box is the most practical.

You can buy a dog's prepackaged first aid kit from the American Red Cross or a commercial company, or you can assemble your own. A list of some things you need to have on hand follows:

- Eye wash
- Eye dropper
- Triple Antibiotic cream
- Plastic tweezers or forceps

- Hydrogen Peroxide
- Pepto Bismal
- Rectal Thermometer
- Mineral Oil
- Bandage Scissors
- Skin wash
- Hydrocortisone cream
- Powdered styptic
- Antiseptic towelettes
- 4" x 4" gauze bandages
- 3 in wide Ace bandages and tape to hold it on
- 4" x 4 yd stretch gauze
- 1 or 2 pairs of latex gloves
- Several zip lock bags, small to medium
- A small comprehensive first aid paperback book and a list of any special instructions your vet may provide.

CHAPTER 9:
Training an Akita or How to Bond with your Akita

Training any dog well is the only way to have a happy dog and a happy home but training an Akita well is a bottom line necessity.

Akitas will behave in a dominant, aggressive manner unless he knows, AND BELIEVES that YOU are the Alpha dog in the pack.

THE VERY BEST GIFT YOU CAN GIVE YOUR NEW AKITA IS VERY THOROUGH AND VERY EFFECTIVE OBEDIENCE TRAINING.

Three ways to teach your Akita basic obedience skills.

There are a number of ways to train an Akita in basic obedience skills.

Advanced obedience, agility and show training, as

well as behavioral corrective training require
further training or consultations.

The most immediate need for your Akita is to teach him to be housebroken and to teach him the basic commands.

One way is to send him away to be trained by a professional trainer and have returned to you a few weeks later.

I would not recommend this "absenteeism training" with any dog, but particularly NOT WITH AN AKITA.

Even if the dog learns well with this trainer and obeys in ways that would impress the most rigid obedience standards, he may never obey you in the same way. If at all.

AND YOU MUST BE THE ALPHA LEADER WITH AN AKITA.

I once had two large Siberian Huskies for neighbors. Their owner was a young man who loved their looks and their "in" status but had no interest in training them.

So he sent them off with an expensive trainer who promised to bring back two well behaved, obedient, charming dogs.

One of the last times I saw was this young man, he was being dragged around, struggling, by these two absolutely wayward huge dogs.

Their obedience was limited to the trainer.

The last thing I heard the young man saying was that he was about to give them away – ostensibly because he was too busy to spend time with them but really because he could not control them.

Without proper training, it is unlikely that these two beautiful dogs will ever find or keep a home. These are the mismanaged dogs that are too often euthanized – perfectly good dogs killed simply because they have not been trained properly.

Here is a fact many dog owners refuse to acknowledge. Without voice-activated obedience commands, they have the equivalent of wild dogs.

You cannot be in denial about your Akita's training. The best person to train your new Akita is YOU and your family.

An Akita needs loving attention combined with the three magic training words: Clarity, Consistency and

131

Patience.

Expect to hear those three words again.

And again.

And again.

Akita Training 101

I say Training 101 because your Akita's first classes are so important in preparing him later for more advanced obedience training.

And, although your dog may be older, this training section can be used to either train or provide your older Akita with a refresher course and perhaps a few new commands.

Once an Akita puppy is three months old, he can attend Puppy Kindergarten.

These are wonderful classes, offered by a great number of trainers, that can start when he is three months old and go on until he is about five or six months old.

They are only one short session once a week and they are FUN.

Puppy kindergarten teaches your dog and you the basic commands and socializes him at the same time.

Socialization at a very young age helps prepare an Akita to be able to live safely with other animals and children.

It is fun for him to meet and play with the other puppies; it is fun for you to meet other dog owners. And it's fun to work your dog for the first time.

Check with your local vets. They know most of the puppy kindergartens and dog trainers in their areas. Better still, they will know their reputations.

Before you enroll your Akita, visit the class when it is in session and see if you like the class for your dog. Check out the trainer in action.

All training classes should be led by a certified dog trainer. You can ask if they have experience training an Akita but don't reject the trainer on that basis alone.

Is the class small enough to permit personal attention by the trainer when needed?

Will the puppies have a little time to play? It is critical to any puppy that the class is at their size and play level.

No trainer should ever encourage physical abuse, including hitting, frightening, yelling at your dog, or throwing small objects at your dog.

No one should ever "dangle" a dog in the air by its leash. That may frighten the dog into submission but it may also frighten him or her so much they are ruined, spirit totally broken, scared hovering animals that pee from fright when they see you.

One clue to a good training program: If your instructor uses the leash and food treats, or a small clicker to help train your Akita puppy, you have a knowledgeable and compassionate trainer.

HOUSEBREAKING YOUR NEW AKITA PUPPY

Since the Akita puppy should be three or four months old before puppy kindergarten class, you will need to housebreak him before then. He can start training at eight weeks old.

You also need to teach him his basic commands.

But first, let's talk about HOW to train your new Akita.

The three words you need to remember when training your Akita are CLARITY, CONSISTENCY AND PATIENCE.

See, we are saying them again.

As for patience, I'll bet it took you almost two years to become "house-broken. " Figure that out in dog years.

In fact, if you think of your new Akita as a toddler of about three years young, it will lessen your frustration and his as you both patiently learn together.

CLARITY: Clear commands make for obedient dogs

I once helped train a dog prepare to become a pet therapy dog. This small dog, a Pomeranian, was a puppy about six months young when he joined a class of large service dogs in training for Canine Companions for Independence.

He was of course the smallest in the class of large

135

Labs. However, that cut him no slack. All service dogs are trained in AKC Good Citizen quality obedience, so this young dog had to follow the same obedience training rules as the larger service dogs.

I almost ruined him before he got started.

I would say, "Come," then before he could come, say something else like, "Come on, you good dog."

I did the same during exercises where he was supposed to be learning how to ignore the distraction of dogs circling around him.

"Stay, come on, be a good boy and stay," I would say to this dog who quickly caught on that I hadn't a clue. And that HE was the Alpha dog in this team.

The wise trainer fortunately quickly realized it was ME who needed training. She helped me learn to say "Come," then shut up and let him come to me.

And then, and only then, give him a tidbit as a reward – or some wild eyed enthusiastic praise.

The training is always for the owner as well as the dog.

Note: Use one word commands, always use the same word, get your dog's attention first by using its name,

136

praise your dog to the skies when he does what you have commanded and give him a tiny treat.

Alternate the treat with enthusiastic praise and petting as he starts to respond to your commands. Intermittent reinforcement works better than the same old, same old.

Incidentally, all dogs love the words, "Good Dog." Don't ask me why, they just perk up when they hear those words. Maybe it's the loving tone that always seems to accompany them.

CONSISTENCY: The mantra for housebreaking and all that follows

Crate Training

You can use a plastic "taxi" as puppy crates are sometimes called to housebreak a dog. It's a great way to train a dog but it takes time. If you have a long weekend coming up, you might arrange to pick up your new Akita at its beginning.

It also takes that special patience mentioned earlier.

But let's talk first about the crate you can buy in any pet supply store and some department stores.

The size is of utmost importance.

A dog will not soil its living space. True so far.

That is, unless the living space is larger than it needs
to be for the dog to settle in. Then, I once sadly
discovered, it will simply move to the rear of the
crate and do its thing. That can be a nasty surprise.

Worse, he's learning the wrong lesson.

So, try to buy a crate that is just slightly larger than
your dog. Forget about letting it "grow into" a large
crate. They are inexpensive and easily replaced for
the Big Grown Up Akita.

A towel can be used as a pad on the bottom of the
crate. Again, follow your dog's lead. Some dogs will
chew on and even eat the pad. If so, take it out. He
won't know the difference. Or at least, he won't go on
strike about it.

And you won't have an emergency visit to the vet
first weeks out.

Now comes the special scheduling and why it is great
if you can arrange for a long weekend to start doing

these housebreaking chores.

While you're housebreaking him, your dog should be taken out of its crate about every two hours (four hours at the Most!) and taken outside or wherever it is you want him to "go."

Praise him for his good deed. Then put back in his crate for another one to four hour session.

Putting a little treat in his crate will help you entice him into going back in. If he resists, push him gently in. Do not take no for an answer. Remember, YOU are the Alpha Dog.

Never leave him in a crate for more than four hours maximum at a time while training him to eliminate.

If you must leave him n the house (Akitas live in the house, not outside) before he is housebroken, fear not. You can easily set up a special place for him using paper training and an inexpensive wooden baby gate.

Note: During the eight hour night, the dog can be left in its crate. He will be lonesome and want you near. Put his crate near your bed so he can hear you breathing.

Paper training for your Akita

While some trainers do not approve of paper training for an Akita, it's actually a good transitional tactic.

Why?

Because paper training is the easiest way in the world to train a puppy where to eliminate. And because once he's paper trained, that training technique can be transferred to the yard.

First, choose a place with a linoleum floor or its equivalent that can be shut off from the rest of the house. A tile floored bathroom or laundry room is perfect.

Then buy an inexpensive baby gate that can shut off the room without closing the door when you want to keep him in the room you've chosen. He can see you but he can't get out.

Now, the paper.

There are wonderful puppy "pee" pads sold just about everywhere that have a chemical scent to entice your puppy to urinate on them. They are soft and white and easily disposable.

However, yesterday's newspaper does just as well. (You can leave one piece with his smell on it from the day before when you change his paper.)

You cover the entire floor with paper. You take him out of the crate and put him in the "paper room." And wait.

When you notice that nice wet spot that says he' s figured out what the paper is for, remove a piece of the newspaper – or puppy pee pad -- farthest from the wet spot.

Each time you see that he has done his thing, notice where and take another piece of paper away. Soon the only place there will be paper on the floor is where he's staked out his "bathroom."

Obviously, paper training for an Akita is only a transitional stage. He needs to "go" outside.

Usually, taking him outside in the morning when he wakes up, after each meal and before bedtime at night will quickly help him become housebroken.

If you've trained him on paper, just stake out an area outside with paper weighted down with rocks and do the removal bit outdoors. He'll already know what to do when you take him out and put him on the paper.

You should also limit the Akita's water and food about an hour or so before his last scheduled trip outside.

How do you know when to take him out?

If he starts to squat or run in circles in the house, he needs to GO OUT.
QUICKLY pick him up and carry him to the outdoors spot you've covered with his usual paper.

When he smells his droppings, he will use that spot to repeat his actions. I once took a piece of his dirty paper from the bathroom outdoors so he would find his smell to tell him where to "do his thing."

Sometimes, a dog will look for other dogs' droppings to inspire him. But taking him to his outdoor bathroom when he is in need is a quick way to train him where to go.

The alternative to the paper training routine is to watch him like the proverbial hawk and every time he starts circling and about to sit, grab him, say NO and carry him outside. Even if he does something in the house, say NO and take him out and show him where he's supposed to go.

Quietly clean up the mess – okay, mutter under you r breath – but don't make a huge fuss about it.

Do not use negative training methods. Hitting him or screaming at him if he urinates or defecates by accident will *not* train him.

Studies have shown that unless you tell him NO within five seconds after he has done either of these things, he will not understand what you mean. He will have forgotten what he did.

Needless to say, pushing his nose in his feces will only teach him fear and humiliation. He really won't understand why. Or what you want of him.

Note: The best way to discourage a repeat of his mistake if you've missed the chance to take him outside is to *TOTALLY IGNORE HIS DEED*. Clean it up without a word and try to catch him before he does it next time.

When an action – good or bad -- is acknowledged by attention, it reinforces it.
Remember the class bully who always got so much attention when he acted out? He kept it up, didn't he?

What about training my Akita to be a guard dog?

Do not use, or let anyone else use or convince you to use harsh, painful methods to try to make your Akita a ferocious guard dog.

If you do, you may find that you have created a "ticking time bomb".

Another very good reason to Just Say No to this ill-advised advisor is that abusing an animal is now a felony in most states, punishable by large fines and imprisonment.

The Akita is *naturally* very protective of his family. Protection of you and yours is in his genes.

And don't think he isn't a good guard dog because he doesn't usually bark. That is an Akita trait. Akitas would crawl close to the ground as they hunted, and never gave their prey any warning!

Because it is so rare, his bark is guaranteed to get your attention!

Special note: If you have adopted an older or adult

144

Akita, it will take more patience, observation and attention to "retrain" him.

You may need the help of a behavior specialist. More about this later.

If you love your dog, protect him from being labeled "dangerous."

Rehabilitating your "problem" Akita

"I had to put him down."

"He had to be put away."

"I had to let him go."

"He had to put to sleep."

All these are euphemisms for killing a dog.

I think we always use them because it is too painful to accept that we are about to kill a companion we had such high hopes for. One we may have come to love. One our children may have come to feel part of the family.

Sometimes it seems there is no other thing to do.

Other times, it is the owner who needs more training to be able to help the dog know what is expected of

145

him.

One young father I know owned a large Rottweiler
before his daughter was born.
He is also an amateur photographer. After his
daughter's birth, he thought it was great fun to take
photos of his 15 month-old child sitting in the
Rottweiler's large crate with the dog.

The dog accepted this and seemed very calm about
the situation.

As the little girl became a toddler, she was taught to
play with the Rottweiler as if the dog and she were
playmates.

One day, the little girl tried to take back a ball and
the dog growled at her.

Immediately, the little girl's mother and father gave
the dog away.

Now, until I spoke to a breeder, I thought, well, of
course. Bad Dog. Dangerous Dog. About to bite the
little girl.

"Not necessarily," said the dog behavior expert.

"The dog was taught that the little girl and he were on the same level. He was not taught that she was above him in the pecking order. So when she took the ball, he was chastising her as he would another dog," she said.

The dog may have needed rehabilitation. This is where the services of a dog behavior psychologist comes in.

Cesar Millan, a dog behaviorist known as the Dog Whisperer who is seen regularly on the National Geographic Channel, specializes in working with what he calls Power Breeds -- large dogs noted for their strength and dominant temperaments.

Cesar's not a trainer as in sit, stand, and stay. His holistic approach is used to rehabilitate pet owners and pets.

"When you make the decision to own one of these (Power Breed) dogs, you must immediately become a committed pack leader," says Millan.

"Once again the needs of all dogs must be fulfilled on a daily basis, but especially for power breeds. This is done through spaying or neutering, and of course, through daily exercise, rules, boundaries, and limitations," says Millan.

And by giving the dog the calm assured guidance of

an Alpha Pack Leader.

If you have behavioral problems with your Akita, your breeder may be able to recommend a good Dog Behavioral Psychologist. It usually only takes one or two conversations or home visits to head you and your dog in the right direction.

For some really neat videos showing Millan working with dogs, their owners, and their problems, see: http://cesarmillaninc/dog-whisperer.php

Basic training for Akitas.

Before every command, get your dog's attention by first using his name. And please remember that teaching him good things happen when he responds to his name is the number one lesson.

Basic commands include:
- Sit
- Stay
- Heel
- Come
- Down
- Off

The command "Leave It" is one of my favorites

though not usually included in basic command lists. Its something picked up at that great service dog course mentioned earlier.

The command "Leave It" is one I recommend to all dog owners. You may save your dog's life with this command.

It is a useful command for dogs who like to pick up and eat stray sharp bones that might injure them, bits of chocolate bars – poisonous to dogs -- on the ground, or other things toxic to him.

One of the most dangerous substances to dogs is anti-freeze. It looks like greenish water on the ground and tastes sweet to your dog. And it is deadly.

A quick "Leave It" could save your dog's life.

Chocolate is another highly dangerous substance to dogs. Unfortunately, chocolate can sometimes be found on the ground. A quick "Leave It" may turn your dog away from the chocolate in time.

Here is how you teach your dog this simple but life-saving command. It is so much fun for your dog that it will seem like a game to both of you.

As soon as he learns "Sit" and "Stay", start on "Leave

It."

Position your dog in "Sit" and then say "Stay."

Back away slowly (facing your dog) and put a treat on the floor about three or four feet from your dog.

When he starts to move towards it, say "Leave It." Hold his collar to stop him from going to his treat without your release word, if necessary.

If he insists on getting the treat before the release word, pick the treat up and end the game for a few minutes. Act disgusted.

Then, after about ten to fifteen minutes later, try again.

Keep your Akita in the Stay position just long enough for you to know he is staying away from the treat because of your command.

Then say, "Okay," or "Go" or whichever release word you've decided to use.

Let him go get the treat and as he eats it, praise him with great enthusiasm.

"Good dog," is a great phrase to use since you don't want to touch him while he is eating.

Akitas are very protective of their food and no one, including children and other pets, should be near him or his food dish while he eats.

He will like to learn this command for obvious reasons. Never let him get the treat without first hearing you release word.

Incidentally, "Leave It" is also useful when he looks like he's just about to snatch the Thanksgiving Turkey off the kitchen counter.

Using a leash and collar to teach your dog to "Heel" and to "Sit."

Most dogs don't like collars or leashes until they become accustomed to them.

Buy a soft woven collar for your dog and make sure it is not too tight. Allow for some growth. If you can put two fingers between it and your dog, that's not too tight. Let him walk around with it on without a leash for awhile.

After he stops trying to pull it off, add a soft woven leash or a skinny round soft leather leash.

Note: Some trainers suggest that you use a "choke collar", a collar that is made of metal chains or, most recently, soft woven fabric with rings at each end. You attach the leash to one of them. As you walk, the dog can be controlled by pulling the collar, thereby putting pressure on his neck.

There are also "prong" collars recommended by some. They release a ring of prongs so that they squeeze his neck a bit as you use the leash to pull. Since I've never seen them used in a training class, I will be referring to the use of a regular collar.

This is your decision to make when you begin training your Akita. One may work better for you than another.

Holding the leash loop in your right hand, with the dog on your left, hold the leash as it crosses your body down near the dog. This lets the dog feel how you move with the leash and keeps him close to your left leg.

Start to move and say "Heel" in a command voice. Since he doesn't yet know what "heel" means, you will have to keep the leash in your left hand close to your body as you move forward. He will feel the slight tug and start to move with you.

You can make a knot in the leash exactly where you need to hold the left part of it to keep a consistency in the way you "lead" the dog and make him aware of your actions and demands. If you let the leash too loose, he will move ahead of you.

An old – fashioned way to prevent this was to step on your dog's foot as he moves forward. Do not do this. A more effective way to show him what to do is to stop, position him in "Sit" position and start again.

After he moves forward with you, praise him, maybe give him a little tidbit, and then keep moving.

Make it a short walk.

Each time you stop, say "Sit" in your command voice. At the same time, you might lift his leash, pulling his front up a bit, and gently push down his haunches at the same time until he is in "Sit" position.

You can also train him to sit on command by holding a small treat in front of his face, a bit higher than his head. As he lifts his head, he will usually drop his butt to the ground. If not, you can help him out with a gentle push on his back haunches.

Immediately praise him as if he just won Best of Show.

You can also teach your dog to "Sit" in the house while off his leash the same way.

Again, don't keep him in training mode for more than five or ten minutes. He'll get bored unless he's in a training class where he feels like he's competing with the other dogs. Even there, he will get a break to just run around and be a dog.

If your Akita does NOT do well in a training class after puppy kindergarten, work with a trainer who will work with you and your dog one-on-one.

The important thing is that he be trained with you as the Alpha in the family and that he be socialized.

A small warning: Trying to socialize your dog-aggressive Akita by taking him to a dog park is an extremely dangerous thing to do. A dog park is stimulating to all dogs, and small dogs as well as large dogs may be considered prey by your dominant Akita. Experienced Akita breeders recommend that Akitas, no matter how sweet and docile they may behave with their families, and even their families' other pets, be kept away from dog parks.

Come and Stay commands

These are learned after he learns the command "sit

and "Stay."

One way to train a dog to "Come" is to use a long expanding leash (one that has a lock you can control) or a long piece of clothesline.

Take your dog outdoors with his expanding leash or rope and either let him run out about six feet or more and "sit", or put him in Sit" position and slowly back off from him. If you back off, do it slowly and not too far. About three feet should do it.

Now, lean towards him and firmly say in a normal tone of voice "Come." Hold a tidbit in your hand he can see if he resists coming to you.

When he responds by running to you, pet him, praise him and give him the tidbit. Repeat this a few minutes each day and he will soon run to you when you say "come."

NOTE: Two secrets about training: Intermittent giving of a tiny treat while training is more effective than always handing it over.

Studies have shown that rats that are given treats only occasionally will work harder to get that one treat.

And hand signals, if incorporated into training, can become another way to say the same thing to a dog.

For instance, say "Stay", and at the same time, hold your hand up like a stop sign. The dog learns to "Stay" on verbal command, and also "Stay" when he sees your hand signal without verbal command. (Hand held up, bent at wrist, palm facing dog's face.)

Eventually, your dog will stay with either command.

Down Command

Like the Sit command, a dog can be taught to lay down using a gentle manipulation of his body as you say "Down."

Have the dog in front of you. As you say "Down" in a firm but natural tone, push gently on his shoulder area. When his body touches the ground, quickly give him a small treat. Give it to him within three seconds so he understands that the treat is for him lying down.

Training tidbits are helpful because they are so small they will not add a lot of weight to your dog. However, try out a few different training tidbits and use the one he wants the most.

Another way to teach your dog "down" is to simply hold a treat in front of his face and slowly lower it so

156

he must go down to get it. As he moves downward, push gently on his shoulder area. He gets the tidbit when he is all the way down.

All training tips are basically simple; what makes them successful is YOUR PATIENCE.

Repetition is the key.

And repetition must be spaced out so that your intelligent Akita doesn't get bored or over-trained in one session

Off, Off, Off Koda!

You and your family have decided that the new sofa is off limits.

"Off" is the command word you need to get him off and keep him off.

As soon as he jumps on the sofa – or bed or whatever you've decided is off-limits, Say "Off" in a firm tone of voice, and lift his paws off the sofa and put them on the floor.

Then, acting as if he obeyed without assistance, praise him for being on the floor. Do not scold him for not doing it at once.

Three important phases of training a dog a new command are making sure he knows what the command means (what do you want him to do?), how to do it,
and that he has pleased you when he's done it.

Do not give him a lot of attention, even negative attention, when he's misbehaving. That reinforces what you DON'T want him to do. Remember the class bully?

Tell him, show him, praise him.

Tell him, show him, praise him.

And always, Clarity, Consistency and Patience.

CHAPTER 10:
Caring for your Older Akita

As your Akita ages, his needs will change. At seven years of age, he will need to start having annual blood and urine tests to check for physical changes or possible illnesses.

Now, he will need an annually physical exam twice a year and maybe have a prescription or two to help him with joint pain or an onset of canine diabetes.

He will need continued teeth care and possibly some advanced professional dental care.

If he hasn't shown indications of having any of the breed related illnesses commonly developed by Akitas, he may do so by now.

He may not see or hear as well and have night blindness, a precursor
of progressive retinol atrophy.

He may feel the heat and cold more intensely.

Now is the time for compassion, continued appreciation, and some minor changes in his diet and lifestyle.

What will you feed him now that he is a senior canine?

Fortunately, that is not a problem. Today, there are formulas devised especially for your senior dog that contain less protein and fats.

Obesity is discouraged in the older dog – while medications that promise to increase flexibility to his joints are common. And pain treatment for dogs with arthritis helps him continue his walks – a little slower perhaps – with you.

Your senior Akita's quality of life now depends on you more than ever.

What can you do to make your senior canine's life better?

You can change his diet to a senior formula; check with your vet for any supplements that might help him have the optimal health he can have; work with your vet to treat whatever illness he might have; make his physical being as comfortable as possible;

and you can help him live life simply yet as closely to his old lifestyle as possible.

Did you eat early then walk together? Keep the same schedule but make the walks shorter and slower.

Make his two meals a day quiet time and top off his water bowl each time you pass it.

Buy or make one of those terrific little three or four step "doggie steps" that allows him to climb right up onto the sofa and down again with no jumping to jar his already fragile joints.

Or, if the steps leading to your front door are too much for Kedo now, put in a small dog ramp.

Maybe he would like one of the newly invented dog pillows fitted with a cold or hot pad.

While you are helping create a predictable stress free schedule, keep him walking and as active as possible. The more active he is, the longer he will be active. Remember the old adage, "Use it or lose it."

CHAPTER 11:
Traveling with your Akita

One of the most pleasant experiences you can have is driving with your dog sitting in back of you, the breeze blowing in the windows, new scenes passing by.

Some dogs take to cars naturally. Others do not.

Either way, all dogs must be acclimated to riding in vehicles. First decide HOW your dog will travel in your vehicle.

These days, you have a wide choice of dog seatbelts, mesh car dividers, crates he can lay in as you zip along, or for small dogs, car seats that raise him to the level of the windows while cushioning his little bottom with sheepskin.

Experts advise that your dog be in the back of the car, directly behind the driver. Most dogs are seen cheerfully window watching in the passenger seat. The seat experts now refer to as the Death Seat.

Wherever you decide he will sit, he first has to want to get into the car.

The first thing to do is to make riding in the car comfortable and void of any anxiety. Dogs get sick in cars mostly because they are having full blown anxiety attacks.

For months, my dog would throw up every time I put him in the car. (He wouldn't get in on his own) Not too much fun for him or me and any other passengers. Fortunately, that ended when I got more information about car sickness and how to help my dog adjust to vehicles.

Behavioral specialists advise that you start off by taking your dog for very short rides, like out of the parking lot and around the block . . . or less. When he gets out of the vehicle, celebrate with lots of praise.

When driving, watch your dog's expression. If he looks like he is getting uncomfortable, pull over quickly and let him walk with you outside the car for a few minutes. Then try again. If he starts to look panicky again, do the same thing. He will eventually calm down; that is the goal. He's throwing up because he is terrified.

Try not to feed him for an hour or so before putting him in the car. That also helps reduce the possibility of him becoming ill in the car.

Take a roll of paper towels and some air refresher like Fabreez with you – unless your dog is allergic to air fresheners.

The important thing is to make as little a fuss about his transgressions in the car as possible. It goes without saying that yelling at him or hitting him for becoming carsick or overly anxious is counter-productive and will not change his behavior. He doesn't know what you want of him.

Sometimes distractions can calm him until he is no longer anxiety in this situation. Some dog owners use their car radio to soothe their pets; others pet their dogs at red lights. One dog owner who travels a lot sings to her dog whenever she sees panic in his eyes. All right. He's calm; he's interested in the scenery; he's fallen asleep on his own towel you've brought for him to lay on. His seat harness is attached to the car's locked seatbelt. Or he's sitting in the back in his crate. And traveling the open road with Suki is as you dreamed it could be.

Note: There is only one safe way to safely transport your animal in the open bed of a truck. ONLY ONE.

You need to have a metal ring soldered in the very center of your truck. Then you attach your dog's

167

chain (yes, metal chain) to the metal ring. The "leash"/chain must be only long enough to allow the dog to stand up away from the edges of the truck bed.

This is the straight scoop directly from the case histories of professional animal cruelty officers. Several shared stories of what happens to dogs who accidentally fall or jump from open truck beds. You do not want to know. Keep your beloved Akita inside your vehicle or follow their instructions.

Longer than daytrips

If your trip is expected to last overnight, or for an extended period of time, you might want to bring some or all of the following things with you for your dog.

large bowl and his food; take as much food as you may need during the entire trip. Dogs do not do well with new foods suddenly thrust upon them. It can upset his stomach and affect his temperament. It could also cause him to throw up or get diarrhea. Ugh.

Traveling is no time to make a lot of changes. He already has a number of them to adjust to during travel.

Pure water: Bring enough gallons with you to last the entire trip. He also needs a drinking bowl. He probably can't drink from a bottle.

Medications and a basic first aid kit. (See the Health chapter). Bring any and all medications he may need. If he gets diarrhea, you will be happy to have your Pepto Bismal with you. Check out the dosage with your vet and take notes before you leave home.

Inoculations: His shots for rabies should be current as well as his usual annual vaccinations. If you are heading into camping in the woods or any where ticks are found, have your dog (and you and anyone else going with you) inoculated for Lyme disease. And take tweezers, antiseptic lotion, and a zip lock bag with you. If you or your dog is bitten by a tick, your vet or physician will want to see the tick.

Note: Before you leave home, you can check with the Center for Disease Control to find out what wildlife and insects (or snakes) are common in that area. Once you make a list, ask your vet to go over it with you and suggest what medications or preventatives you might need with you.

In any wooded areas, it's wise to keep your dog near you.   Wild animals can and have attacked pets.

Adequate identification is imperative for your dog when traveling. Please see the Identification section of this book for micro-chip information.

Note: Heat is a big issue when you are traveling. A dog, like a child, must NEVER be left in an automobile – even with the windows "cracked" a bit – in very warm or hot weather. Temperatures inside an automobile can reach 150°F in minutes! That will kill your precious Akita. If you need to leave the car, leave someone outside of the car with your dog. Take turns walking him a bit each time you have to stop.

If you and your dog are traveling alone, take advantage of official rest areas, drive through eating places and open air picnic-type restaurants that permit dogs.

Rest areas usually have restrooms, fast food shops, water and gas. This is a good opportunity to stretch your legs, including your dog's.

Crates: Take your pet's usual carrier with you even if he is going to be harnessed in the car. They come in handy when your dog needs to be separated from children or other animals as well as when he needs to have a place to retreat to when he's tired and wants to be alone. Leave the crate door open and he will go into his sanctuary on his own.

His medical and vaccination records: If he needs emergency medical care on the road, they will be very helpful to a new temporary vet.

Motels/Hotels: Check ahead for motel and hotel arrangements: even motels and hotels noted for taking animals may have size or breed limitations. Then again, if they are in a slump, they may relax the rules and be happy to have your dog. Always ask but be honest. I've seen Pit Bulls sneaked into motels that do have dominant breed restrictions, only to be asked to leave IMMEDIATELY.

His favorite toy/blanket/towel/sleeping pad: Like a child's things, these are pacifiers for your dog. A happy serene dog is a good traveling companion.

Traveling by plane

Since your Akita will not be permitted in the cabin, you need to prepare to ship him by plane. That is complicated by the fact that each airline has its own policies regarding the transporting of live cargo.

So, if you ship your dog by air, check the airlines you are using and adhere very strictly to their guidelines. Try to get a non-stop flight; it's faster and the dog only has to be placed on board once. In addition, he will not be subjected to long periods in the cargo space or on the tarmac while the plane sits for long periods.

His crate size, his weight, his size all will come into play as you work with the airline to ship your dog, whether or not you are with him.

For airline's policies, see the website for your
airline(s) of choice.

Pet Couriers – Are They For You?

There are animal courier companies world-wide who
offer different services, all designed to deliver your
animal to you by ground transportation.

Professional pet couriers are bonded and trained to
ensure that your pet arrives healthy and happy. The
best ones use air-conditioned vehicles, regular
exercise breaks, and hotels that cater to pets. They
are dedicated to delivering your animal by ground
transportation so that he – and you – are relieved of
the trauma of airline travel for your dog.

It is recommended that you always ask for references
and talk to their former clients -- and really listen
"between the lines."

To find a bonded and licensed professional pet
courier, see the Independent Pet and Animal
Transportation Association at
http://www.ipata.com/

General rules for airline travel

Have your dog checked for any possible problems
and have his vaccinations brought up to date if you

have not already done so. Do all this about a month before he is going to travel by plane.

NOTE: If you are going from one state to another, your dog will need a state-issued certificate for interstate travel completed by a qualified veterinarian. Ask your vet about this at least a month before traveling.

Do not sedate him for his flight. Dogs do not respond well to sedatives. In flight, that tendency could be further aggravated.

He must be in a crate large enough for him to stand up and turn around in it. The crate must have a pad for his physical protection and to contain his urine and feces. A favorite bit of your clothing could help him feel less abandoned.

The crate should have the handler's name pasted on the top. Include any food he may need taped on the crate's top as well. Write Live Dog – This Side Up on the top of the crate in huge letters – and then pray.

Crates must have water and food trays attacked to the inside of their doors. You can buy these when you buy his crate.

Have his nails cut before he travels so he won't catch them on his cage or something else in the cargo space.

Have a collar and identification on him; microchip him before the flight. I repeat: Collars can come off. A micro chip is forever.

Before you leave the airport or get on the airplane, check that he is actually loaded on the plane. Be persistent. Be nice but take everyone's name.

Pet Travel agencies and Travel Clubs

These days, the attitude towards traveling animals is rapidly changing. Hotels and motels are actually courting pet owners and their pets. Airlines are noticing that pets mean Money. Even some – rare but very welcome -- disaster shelters are changing their no pet attitudes.

Pets are now a burgeoning industry popping up with all kinds of new places, things and services for our pets. Even yoga classes are being held for dogs and owners. And they look like fun.

You can take your dog to the beach, the mountains, a doggie spa, a doggie boutique -- and even on a cruise! Pets are in!

That said, two appealing services popping up on the

Internet lately are dog travel agencies and dog travel clubs. Both operate the same as the human versions but it's Mr. and Ms. Pets that are their focus. One or the other may be helpful to you and your Akita.

Again, always ask for references you can check.

CHAPTER 12:
A Dozen Questions to
Ask an Akita Breeder

1. Have you ever produced dogs with a
   health problem?
   *If they say no, listen to the rest
   carefully. Above all, you want and
   need an honest breeder.*

2. How long have you been breeding the
   Akita?
   *The longer the breeder has been in
   business, the better although it is no
   guarantee that this is the breeder for
   you.*

   *Visit several professional breeders
   before you buy your Akita. And ask
   for references of several folks who
   have bought their Akitas from them
   – THEN CALL THEM. Listen
   carefully to what they say. **And
   how they say it**. Follow up with
   questions to clarify what you are*

177

hearing if something in their voice
alerts you to more that they are
NOT saying.

3. How do you socialize your Akita puppies?
   *The more good experiences with
   dogs and people an Akita has during
   his early months, the better his
   temperament will be.*

4. Do you show your dogs?
   *This is an important sign that the
   breeder knows about Akitas and has
   good breeding lines. This is
   important even if you do not plan to
   show your dog.*

5. Do you belong to an all-Breed club, like
   the American Akita Club or the Japanese
   Akita Club?
   *This is again a sign that the breeder
   is likely to have sophisticated
   knowledge about the Akita and good
   breeding lines.*

6. I would like to see the parents and/or
   siblings of the dog we are considering
   buying.
   *Pedigreed papers do not necessarily
   guarantee the quality of the specific
   dog you are buying; only that it is a
   purebred dog.*

It is highly recommended that, in addition to these questions, you meet a number of Akitas, get involved in an Akita club, and go to shows that feature Akitas BEFORE YOU GET YOUR AKITA.

Note: Legitimate Akita breeders do not sell to pet shops; puppy mills and back yard breeders do. The folks that run puppy mills are not interested in good bloodlines or breeding for temperament – or the health of their animals.

The same caveat goes for ads you see in the newspaper from folks who are selling back yard bred dogs. They do not do selective breeding for the best qualities of the breed, including breeding for temperament. Ask for written guarantees of good health if you decide to do this.

Buying through an Internet Puppy Finding site: I ran across several recently, including one ad that read "New and second hand dogs." Enough said.

I strongly recommend against brokering your dog through a stranger ("we will ship the dog anywhere in the United States"), nor should you buy from someone who simply uses the AKC and only the AKC as their drawing card – registering with the AKC is

not a guarantee of quality. It's only a guarantee that
the dog was registered.

It's true, buying a well-bred Akita from an accredited
professional Akita breeder may cost more in the
beginning but it can be a huge bargain in vet fees and
continued personal satisfaction with your dog.

7. May I see the American Kennel Club
    registration papers?
    Do not take no for an answer. If they
    offer excuses instead, walk away from
    that breeder. Even though the
    American Kennel Club registration is
    just a registration, the papers can tell
    you something, and that may be
    helpful to you.

8. Next, ask for OFA and CERF certificates
    to prove that their Akitas have been ex-
    rayed for hip dysplasia and deemed free
    of eye diseases. If this has not been done
    or, if they say a vet examined the dog and
    said he's fine but they have nothing in
    writing, ask for the vet's telephone
    number and call him yourself to check on
    this. Akitas are prone to these diseases.
    See Question 1.

9. If they do not offer, ask them for his or
    her vaccination papers. They should
    include documented proof that the dog
    has received Parvo, Lept, Distemper and
    all other preventive medications and

wormed for ascarids. In writing.

I once had a friend buy a purebred dog from a pet shop (mistake!) where the owner swore the dog had been wormed, had his vaccinations, etc. Fortunately, she took the puppy to a vet within 48 hours. The poor puppy was actually in very bad shape and much younger than said. As the vet said, "He has every kind of worm there is. He's too young to have been taken from his mother."

And then "Do you trust he's had his vaccinations?"

These things happen with unethical breeders and puppy mill dogs all the time. Insist on written proofs. (She paid to have him treated and vaccinated and they lived happily ever after.)

10. What should I feed my dog and how often?

A good breeder will not only give you written instructions in the information and vaccination packet she will give you, but send you off with the right food for your new Akita.

11. Ask to watch the puppy you are

considering buying for awhile before finalizing any sale. Is he a happy puppy with playful ways? Is he relaxed and comfortable with his litter mates?

Know your puppy a bit before you take him home. I've said this before but a dog that you don't like after you get him home is a tragedy for you and an even worse tragedy for the dog.

12. Does the breeder offer written guarantees of his health? Ask before you buy: What do you do if the dog has problems shortly after we take him home? Will you replace him?

All promises must be in writing. This is business. Separate the cute puppy in your mind from the business end. A good show dog can cost thousands. A good companion Akita can cost $1500 or more, depending where the breeder is located.

Note: This is business. After you settle the important financial and other business details to your satisfaction, go wild and hug and kiss and rave about your new Akita to your heart's content. But first know that good business is good insurance.

BONUS CHAPTER:
Let's Play! Tricks to Teach your Akita

Teaching an Akita tricks and games are fun ways for you to bond with this extremely bright dog. Some really easy to teach and easy to learn tricks include Crawling, Jumping through a Hula Hoop, and Dancing Dog.

When considering tricks or games to teach your Akita, keep in mind that this little 20 pound puppy will one day be a very large dog with a lot of weight. Games or tricks that build on the dog's natural agility are the most appropriate to consider.

If you use a ball in any of your games, please use a very large one like a soccer ball or basketball, never a tennis ball or its equivalent in size. Your dog can choke or accidentally swallow a small ball. But he will have a ball with a large ball!

Your Akita can start learning tricks as soon as he's mastered "Sit,"

"Stay" and "Down".

Crawl

Hold a small treat in your right hand. Position him in the Down position and say "Stay". Then put the small treat on the floor in front of his nose and drag it in front of him while saying "Crawl." With your left hand, push down gently on his back haunches while you say "Crawl" so he knows he is not to get up.

If you practice this with your Akita three or four times each evening for several evenings, he is likely to surprise you and crawl as soon as you say 'Crawl' and before you've put the treat on the ground!

Make sure to give him his reward within seconds right after he's crawled a short distance. After he's demonstrated that he knows the word "Crawl" and what it means, you can ask him to crawl longer distances upon command. Soon he will do it without the immediate reward.

Jumping Through a Hula Hoop

This is fun and easy to teach.

Buy a hula hoop that is large enough for him to pass through easily. (As your dog gets larger, you may have to search the discount stores for a larger hoop)

Position him in the "Sit" position and tell him to

186

"Stay."

Walk away slowly a few feet, and hold the hula hoop so one part touches the floor. Hold a small treat in your free hand on the side of the hoop nearest YOU. Then call JUMP to the dog and entice him to WALK through the hoop to get the treat.

Give it to him, even if he hesitates and needs to be called several times. Many dogs are afraid of going through a hoop at first. That's why you keep it on the ground.

When he begins to show he is okay with walking through the hoop, you can start lifting it slightly off the ground and saying JUMP as you entice him with the treat. Then higher. His body language will tell you how high he will jump and where his comfort level ends. What a fun show off kind of trick!

For a roundup of some great and easy to learn dog tricks, see
www.geocities.com/Colosseum/loge/4844/TRICKS.HTML

10434460R0

Made in the USA
Lexington, KY
23 July 2011